Soccer Mind

Raise Your Game With Mental Training

Copyright Mind Training Arena, November 2010

ATTENTION

The information here is intended for people in good health. The ideas, suggestions and techniques here are not a substitute for proper medical advice. Anyone with medical problems of any kind should consult a medical practitioner. Any application of the ideas, suggestions or techniques here are at the readers sole discretion.

This publication contains the authors opinion in the subject matter covered herein. The author makes no warranty of any kind for any particular purpose. The author is not liable or responsible to any person or entity for any consequential, incidental or special damage caused or alleged to be caused directly or indirectly for the information contained within.

All rights reserved. You do not have the right to auction, reprint, resell, re-distribute or transmit in any form Soccer Mind by any means. You may not give away, sell, share or circulate Soccer mind or any of its content in any form without the prior written permission of both Mind Training Arena and the author PAUL M MAHER MA except short pieces for review purposes.

This copy of Soccer Mind you have purchased is for your own personal use. If this is an ebook purchase, they are protected worldwide under international copyright and intellectual property law, the same as printed books, recorded material and other literary works. You are welcome to copy onto CD-ROM or other storage media as backup for your own personal use.

Contents

Contents	iii
Kick Off	v
Introduction	viii
For Coaches	1
The Player – Coach Relationship	4
A Players Evolution	6
State Control	10
Your Mind	12
What About You?	15
Belief	17
Imagination	20
Self-talk	26
Perfectionism	29
The Inner Critic	32
Re-programme Your Self-Image	34
Master Your Emotions	37
Anchoring	39
Pressure	44
Anger & Psyching	47
Breathing	50
Relaxation	52

Rest	56
Soft Eyes	58
Creative Questions	61
Goals	64
Reframing	67
Internal Conflict	69
Motivation	72
Mirroring	76
The Inner Smile	78
Relationships	80
Time Management	84
Fear (False Evidence Appearing Real)	87
Thermometer	91
Spinning	93
Swish	95
Tapping	97
Time Line	100
Pain Control	102
Injuries & Illness	107
Simulation Training	111
Soccer Scrap Book	114
Superstitions	116
Daydream	118
Full Time	120
Bibliography	122
Notes	123
Self-Hypnosis for Soccer	124

Kick Off

"Every single day I wake up and commit myself to becoming a better player!"
Mia Hamm

THIS book is written for players of all levels as a practical guide for them to get the maximum benefit out of their soccer, so they can perform consistently with excellence. My research had found only a little dedicated to the mental skills training of soccer, so my wish is this book will receive favourable comments and interest of what is a motivating, thought provoking and performance changing book.

When I left school I played for a couple of amateur clubs until I went to sea and represented the ships I served on. Always having an interest in fitness, I studied physical culture in the 1980's and started my career in health as a gym manager then becoming a REPS Level 3 exercise professional and expanding into sports therapy where I worked with a couple of semi-professional clubs.

Now I am a Clinical Hypnotherapist with an MA in Sport Psychology and at the time of writing, I am furthering my qualifications by studying for a PhD in Sport Motivational Science. I have spent a fair number of years learning and understanding how the mental side of sport affects performance and most certainly, enjoyment.

Most of the knowledge within the soccer community on the mind in sport performance has come from research undertaken in recent years.

Most professionals, followed by an increasing large number of recreational players now better understand how to improve confidence, belief, motivation, behaviour and master their emotions. Many professional clubs now include a sport psychologist on their medical staff.

The purpose of this book is to teach you how to change the way you think, show you tools to achieve goals and success in soccer by reaching your full potential, if that is what you truly desire. Although only one player in a season will ever become European Footballer of the Year, this book can help you become the heart and soul of your team.

The techniques in this book come from Neuro Linguistic Programming (NLP) commonly referred to as 'the science of success' developed in the mid-seventies by John Grindler, a university lecturer of linguistics and Richard Bandler, a computer programmer, along with sport psychology and ideas from my own sport experiences and hypnosis study.

NLP is steadily becoming recognised for its tools and approaches which benefit the sportsperson in reaching quick and lasting changes and so achieve a successful mindset. By the time you have read this book, you will know some powerful methods to create positive change in your game, or those you coach.

NLP has stood the test of time. Different techniques will work for different people, in different circumstances, at different times, so be open and willing to experiment. There is more than one way to deal with a particular challenge, so take any immediate failure as feedback, adapt it, or simply use another technique. With NLP there is an abundant opportunity to use several approaches which will address a particular concern within soccer, or your life.

The term sports psychologist, understood by most people in the sport industry, or psychologist in any field, may intimidate some soccer people. Traditions go back a long way, so new ideas are often frowned upon. Twenty years ago acupuncture was laughed at, now it's a fully accepted therapy. I feel the recent titles of 'mental skills coach' or 'performance enhancement coach' are far more appropriate and will be accepted more easily by soccer players as someone trained to guide them how to use the resources of their mind more effectively and gain a winning attitude.

This is very much a 'how to' book. Techniques are explained step-by-step so you can use them effectively. Its possible to do them all by yourself, although some may have a greater impact with someone guiding you through the process, or as a coach, you can use these techniques with your players. Its best for you to refer to them often to develop the necessary competence and refresh your memory, just like you would to develop a physical skill. Being in sport, you should realise the importance of practice, practice, practice. Also consider that by re-reading this book or sections of it frequently, you will gain something new and absorbing each time.

As the word 'soccer' is now understood worldwide as opposed to the British term 'football' and since both terms are used identically, I have decided to use 'soccer' throughout for ease of reference.

Enjoy.
Paul M Maher MA

INTRODUCTION

"A lot of football success is in the mind. You must believe you are the best and then make sure that you are."
BILL Shankly

WELCOME. I want to share with you techniques that will motivate you to success in your soccer, teach you strategies that have helped many players break through their imagined limitations and control your thinking, so you can play the game others only dream.

Throw away any limitations forever, the quality of your game will catapult you to new heights. After all, the achievements of one player can energise and inspire the whole team.

Soccer is a great game to grow and evolve. Remember as a child the excitement of unwrapping your first soccer boots? It won't take you long to read this book, but the techniques you learn will serve you in your football career and beyond. Your playing career can be over before you know it, you owe it to yourself to have a stormer.

Let me answer that question ... what's it all about? Mental skills training and sport psychology are not modern concepts, they have been around for as long as sports have been played and are as much about mental attitude as solid technique. It now plays an increasing role in shaping a players behaviour and performance.

NLP emerged about thirty years ago as a way to identify how people regulate their behaviours unconsciously and if required, re-programme their mind. Handy techniques taught here guide you toward powerful, positive change. The mind is the most important body part you can train, here I'll show you how to reach full potential.

As a human, you have an incredible mind that can sometimes get wired up in a way that is not useful for some situations you find yourself in. The subconscious acts in a literal, even naïve way. As its non-judgemental, it will absorb a bad idea as much as a good one. Culture, family, peer pressure, a bad coach, all teach ways that sometimes just are not useful for what you want to achieve.

If you are cynical, believe learning is boring, think this is all weird new-age stuff, we need to have a chat. It does work. Hundreds of therapists like myself and thousands of clients say it does work. There are poor therapists about, as there are poor players, so if you or a colleague have tried something like this before and failed, get over it! Sorry to be so blunt, but doom mongers and nayers will never become better players.

This book is like having me sit down with you and go over, step-by-step, exactly how to do the techniques. The goal of this book is to help you get greater control of yourself and soccer by planting positive suggestions in your mind. The secret to successful soccer is very simple, do something ... anything at all! Even if you mess up on the training field you will be wiser for the experience. Be responsible enough to take action, that's what separates winners from losers.

Use this book as an interactive tool you can dip into, to challenge, excite, inspire and teach. Do not underestimate the methods, you may find them invaluable. If you consider a technique you find not to you're liking, simply find another you can adjust so it suits you're needs, there will be a more exciting one for you on another page.

Allow yourself some quiet space and time to go through these techniques properly. It can all start with one technique and it will start by knowing that technique well. Do not attempt to go all out to learn them all right away. Learn one then extend your range. Even the simple act of doing a minor one can get you moving onto others.

I have made examples of game situations, but you are free to use them as a template which can be adapted to suit you're needs. You have to put the time in to learn and use these methods, but what you are about to learn will help you begin making a wave of changes, now, on this first day. Chances are you will be bitten by the bug as you find confidence grow. Excited? You should be. These methods can rock you to you're core. They can also affect other areas of life. Just sit back, put your feet up and enjoy what I am going to teach you. It starts here ...

For Coaches

"The measure of who we are is what we do with what we have."
VINCE Lombardi

GETTING the best from players is one of the greatest skills needed by any coach. There is a breadth of variation of players, from difficult to complex, sensitive to laid back. For each, you must know which individual buttons to push and at the same time blend them all into a cohesive team unit for it to blossom.

How well you communicate depends entirely on the players response, which means you alone are responsible for how they understand you. Pay attention to the words you use so that you're thoughts, language and communication becomes crystal clear. There are a number of steps to the methods here, so for the benefit of coaches, be they soccer coaches, mental skills coaches, team managers, or parents, here are the keys:

Explain the process to your player or players.

Establish where they are with a particular mental attitude and where they, or you, want them to be. This is best served by using a scale of 0 – 10, with 0 being nothing and 10 being very high. Taking 'anxiety' for example, when a young player is about to make his first team debut in a packed ground, 0 will be nothing, very calm and prepared, while 10 will be extremely anxious, with all the variants in between. Having performed one of the techniques, you can then use the scale of 0 – 10 again to test if the young player's anxiety level has reduced.

You need to know is it absolutely right to change the players thinking, by ensuring there will only be good, ethical consequences to come from making a change to their mindset. This is best by asking useful questions:

What is the purpose of this change?
What will the player lose, or gain by it?
What will happen if they make the change?
What will happen if the player does not make the change?

Go on to perform the technique.

Check the technique has worked and your player has improved, remember the scale of 0 – 10.

Future pace. This is asking your player to imagine a future situation which previously would have created the issue and notice how they now feel about it. Repeat this as often as you feel until your player is convinced their attitude has changed for the best.

Mental skills training is something you do **WITH** a player, not **TO** a player.

Pay attention to any non-verbal communication the player is giving. Is their voice tone, facial expression and body language in accord to their verbal responses?

Be aware, although it is rare, but some players may have repressed or traumatic memories which are beyond your ability to change and may be best dealt with by a qualified therapist. Some NLP techniques are quite powerful and can have a greater impact on players than you realise. Do they have a history of mental illness or depression? Are they on medication or have a history of epilepsy? If in any doubt, DO NOT work with them.

The biggest factor which prevents a coach involved with children and youth teams from enjoying their role is parents. Sometimes unintentionally, the parents rock the boat because they are emotionally involved in their children's welfare. The parents are convinced their child is the best thing to ever happen to the team so will often challenge the coach regarding team selection and game plan.

Also be aware that parents will often try to impose their own motivations, past regrets and vanished dreams upon their children.

Although time consuming, the coach should meet with parents as near to the start of the season as possible to outline goals and for the children to enjoy their soccer experience without necessary concentrating on competitive aspects.

Some coaches will tell a player when something is wrong, but may not give advice on how to correct it. Comments like "you should have done better" puts some players on a long, lonely road. Acknowledge progress and give positive feedback, it motivates, it makes players feel good and improves team spirit.

Pep talks, pumping the team up, last minute changes, complicated instructions just before kick off can all be an obstruction to a players mental preparation. Usually they are only a stress release for the coach. Players, especially at the higher levels know what to do. Yes, players always appreciate encouragement or reassurance on the build up to an important game. After that, most will prefer to be left alone to concentrate during the final minutes before going onto the pitch. Let them know you are available if they need you, then give them freedom to focus on their performance.

Competent coaches will have a great influence on the lives of their players. They are masters of communication and building team spirit. Good coaches care. They support their players, especially if a player is suffering a loss of form, personal setbacks, or injury. They challenge their players to become the best they can be in a positive and respectful manner which will help them grow. They give players the confidence to believe in themselves and their ability by making their players feel valued.

A player can be influenced by a clinical sport psychologist or mental skills coach trained in valuable hypnotic contributions, as these methods can enable change for players who need quick results. Sport hypnosis can offer help for a more positive attitude and adopt psychological qualities which will maintain motivation, give greater discipline in training habits and cure issues such as anxiety, self-esteem, anger, resentment and substance abuse.

One needs the other …

THE PLAYER – COACH RELATIONSHIP

"It's a fine thing to have ability, but the ability to discover ability in others is the true test."
Lou Holtz

In soccer there can be many add-on relationships. The player-parent, player-teacher, player-spouse, player-fan. All can all have an impact on a players performance. The player-coach base should be recognised as being especially crucial.

A players and their coach must develop a relationship based in terms of appreciation, commitment, cooperation, dependence, trust and respect for each other. Overall, the player-coach relationship is a dynamic and sometimes complex process, nevertheless it provides the means by which coaches and players needs are expressed and fulfilled.

Historically, coaching has been preoccupied with enhancing players physical, technical and tactical skills. The coach is a major force in promoting the development of a player physically and even more so these days, psychological, as positive mentoring and support go to create a near perfect working relationship. Positive player growth will develop through empathy, honesty, support and acceptance.

Soccer coaching implies achievement. The performance of both coach and player is shown as being either successful or not. A coach should be able to listen as well as talk. Good communication promotes the development of knowledge and understanding. A successful and effective coach – player relationship will invariably have positive outcomes for the player in terms of psychological health and well-being along with performance.

When giving instructions, not only should the coach make those instructions crystal clear, it should be explained to the players why something is being done so they have a clearer understanding and feel part of the plan.

In contrast, various elements can lead to conflict. Put-downs, critical, sarcastic comments undermine a players confidence. An ineffective or dysfunctional relationship will be marked by deceit, lack of interest, lack of commitment, remoteness, even antagonism and abuse. Ethical and professional issues that are associated with codes of conduct to protect players and coaches run a risk of being breached. Misunderstandings may develop if the coach fails to accurately understand the players intentions or emotions.

A perfect working relationship involves an ability or even desire to understand the other persons meaning and feelings with a strong, improving mutual liking, trust and respect. Emphasis is placed on how behaviours are perceived by the player and coach and their impact on outcomes such as satisfaction, self-esteem besides game performance.

The task of a coach in developing effective relationships that the players can use for growth and development is a challenging one because it is a measure of the growth they have achieved in themselves. This implies a responsibility on the part of coaches in that they must continually strive to develop their own potentials, as this will be reflected in the maturity and growth of both coach and player.

Lets look at the lifespan of a soccer player …

A PLAYERS EVOLUTION

"You have to expect things of yourself before you can do them."
MICHAEL Jordan

THROUGHOUT a soccer players career, there will be many transitions ranging from playing at school in their first pair of boots, to eventually retiring from the game and perhaps going into coaching. Players at all levels, professional or recreational, may take these transitions in their stride, or have a hard time accepting them. Techniques in this book may help overcome these transitions.

So, lets consider the evolution of a soccer professional, of course this does not represent an exact list and depends on the structure of the country, league or club.

The child will begin playing and maybe representing school normally around the six to eleven age group. Sometimes a personal interest is shown or because an influential adult has given encouragement. Here, it is best for the child to gain experience at the skills of the game and any game result should not matter so much. Especially before the age of eight or nine, the child has a limited concept of the modern world around them, thinking they are the centre of that world, so making it difficult at an early age to integrate into a team sport.

As the child gets older, the child feels a strong need to have their worth confirmed or appreciated. If parents and coaches encourage and are not too demanding of their child's performance, it will become a positive development in the child's self-esteem.

Joining a soccer academy. Into teens now and reactions are much more emotional. The teenager is a confused mess, remembering childhood experiences while looking toward the future, without any reassurance for the present while searching for self-identity. There is a contradiction going on in their mind stemming from disagreement with adults and a desire to also be like them. In youth soccer, when important games come around, the teen will think more on the difficulty of the game and the opposition, than their own physical ability. Avoidance can be an antidote with complaints of feeling ill and any small injuries take on a bigger importance as an excuse not to participate. Promising players may even give up soccer completely to escape their perceived pressure.

Signing on as a junior by a professional club and progressing through the clubs youth, B and A teams into the reserves. There can be conflict with adult authority as the player wants to make his own decisions regarding technique or tactics and may find it hard to accept the position chosen for him on the playing field. Finding a role model or mentor may ease troubles. It is rewarding for the teenager to be accepted and liked by his team mates.

A show of promise brings selection to represent county or country as a junior player. By now, the player cannot accept any limitations on technique and will work exceedingly hard to master any weakness in order to improve.

Signing a professional contract to become a full-time player. Our player will begin to make sacrifices to become more competitive, looking to fill a role in life which needs to be satisfied. Hard training and frequent selection disappointments make some consider their role in his soccer world.

Each transition brings with it new status which will be answered positively or negatively. At any stage a club may decide they no longer require a young players services. It may not be because the player is not good enough, a small club may not be able to afford to keep them. Some players may be lucky and move onto another club, perhaps on a free transfer. Others, without the right quality may still experience a rewarding amateur or semi-pro career by going into non-league soccer, or go into coaching at an early age. Some may never play again, having all their dreams shattered.

For the new professional, perhaps living far from home may create a certain amount of stress. New relationships may become negative experiences, caused by new acquaintances who will try to benefit from the players position rather than out of true friendship. Often the local press is ready to report on any behaviour as they begin to cultivate their own image. Scandal, no matter how exaggerated, sells newspapers.

Breaking into the first team, perhaps by first making appearances as a substitute. Players in this situation are frequently under pressure from coaches, supporters, the media and team mates which, in some cases, goes to increase the players fear of failure.

Becoming established in the first team, or being left on the bench for extended periods through rotation. Now prepared to take risks and be impulsive. This may also create a lack of motivation and lapses in concentration, so it is important for players to continue to work hard at the physical demands of competitive soccer, additionally, with personalised psychological methods that will overcome the negative factors and enhance sporting performance.

Being chosen to represent country at under 21 level. Becoming more sure of life's direction and will begin to make plans how to accomplish further goals in life. Sometime in the near future if not already, commitments regarding marriage and family come along.

Winning a major trophy. It is possible for a player from the lower leagues to reach promotion to a higher level at a particular point in their career. Older players concede when they won a major trophy at a younger age, they did not then appreciate it as much as when they became more experienced or feeling emotionally what they have achieved.

Now becoming a full international and seasoned pro, even club captain. Old enough now to know what they should do to keep playing at the highest level possible. Always in the squad now when fit and want to play every game.

Becoming a senior player and already a role model or mentor for junior players. By now running the first ten metres in their head. Risk-taking declines with a cautious fear of failure. As the player realises he is getting older, maybe no longer the clubs star player, it can upset his frame of mind. Perhaps changes at boardroom level or coaching decisions may de-motivate him. However, players over thirty, who still maintain their fitness and enthusiasm can give a great deal to their team from their knowledge and experience.

Slowing down and making 'cameo' appearances as playing is rationed now and spending longer on the bench. A transfer to a lower club is likely. For a player who has experienced success, there is a danger that they can no longer find stimulation or motivation. Self-image has changed and becoming more aware of that now. A phenomenon known as 'the hypnosis of social conditioning' comes into play. What this means is the player is already programmed to expect his body to begin to break down and wear out. Consequently, as he gets older, the expectation becomes a reality. The good news is there is nothing in medical science saying someone's body will fall apart after the age of 35.

Retirement is staring him in the face as he misses more games than he plays. He may start to take 'another look' at career, home, even his partner and may become more self-interested. Once a soccer career has gone, it creates a void in life with a feeling of helplessness and doubt. Self-image and confidence suffer and he is searching for a safety net when he is no longer playing. The big question on his mind is "what am I going to do?"

Retiring players still have a lot to offer. They can contribute knowledge to younger players and become involved with the youth set up if the club has one to effectively become a role model and mentor to juniors. This passion can itself create new opportunity, perhaps leading to coaching, leadership positions, teaching, writing, counselling or public speaking.

Attending various coaching courses to stay in the game if not already qualified as his soccer career is almost over. He takes a coaching position with a smaller club and if successful and wise, begins to work his way up to higher leagues. As he heads into his fifties, he could start to settle down from renewed energy and a fresh zest for life.

But watch State Control …

STATE CONTROL

"At a football club, there's a Holy Trinity. The players, the manager and the supporters. Directors don't come into it. They are only there to sign the cheques."
BILL Shankly

EMOTIONS run high in soccer. These days it has become more business-minded, its trendy now for corporations to invest in a club, either using their vast millions for a top side, or a local butcher or engineering firm sponsoring the kit for a youth team. A new chairman can be the best thing that ever happened to a club, or the worst. Once a club reaches company status, it wants to sell merchandise, wants to be seen as forward thinking, a stylish, modern corporate body seeking a solid media image. This brings expectation from chairmen, the board of directors and shareholders. A club which is in business does not function through sentiment.

The supporters want their team to accomplish something through a hard fought season. They are desperate to see their heroes win honours. They also have their expectations and follow a ritual every weekend which for some fans, becomes a religious experience.

Coaches, referee's, club and association officials, sponsors and agents all have an involvement. But it's the players who invest their time and energy to accomplish success, either at club level or personal success.

With so much being at stake for so many people around the globe, this need for success leads to strong emotions and various psychological implications for everyone involved. This can be shown by sobbing uncontrollably for a missed penalty to throwing tea cups across the changing room, sheer elation from winning the World Cup or near suicide for losing it.

Many players find themselves in positions on and off the pitch when they are in a 'right state' before or during a game instead of being in 'the right state' and so unable to perform effectively, or worse, embarrass themselves and their club. A bad referee decision can make some players see red. We will take a look at problems such as anger and perfectionism and how to deal with them later on.

For the majority of experienced players in the top leagues, they are more likely to assume any nervousness as adrenalin and motivation to perform well more so than players in the lower leagues. Having said that, lets not forget the many 'giant killers' of the FA Cup who were able to beat much superior opposition because they reached a level of performance intensity far more so then the 'big team' could.

The mood enhancement techniques you will learn here will teach you valuable tools and approaches to use so you will be able to manage confidence and energy level's, or help the players you deal with, especially before and during an important game.

Lets look at the workings of the mind ...

Your Mind

"Behind every kick of the ball there has to be a thought."
DENNIS Bergkamp

EVERY stadium, every new formation, every team decision ever made began with just one thought. You should appreciate by now that what you focus on, you get more of, so the thoughts and the words you use need to be directed to produce positive direction. What you focus on is what you get, so if you think you are tired, you will become so. Imagine how that thought can affect you in a cup final when the ninety minutes are nearly up and you are facing extra time!

Circumstances have a bearing on you such as weather, ground conditions, stadium atmosphere or the importance of the game. When you simplify everything down to its basics, there is no difference between defending a corner in the first minute of the game or defending a corner in the last minute. The difference is your response to the situation. Its not what happens that is so important, but rather how you perceive it which is down to your mental attitude.

By understanding how your mind works you will be able to utilise its power and get the most out of yourself or those you coach. Its often said we use less than ten percent of our mind so most of its enormous latent power is still unknown to medical research.

The mind has two parts, the conscious mind and the subconscious mind, also known as the inner mind, or unconscious mind which is a mistake as its not 'unconscious.' Some spiritual believers also claim we have a super-conscious mind.

The conscious mind consists of approximately 10% of your whole mind. It functions in a state of active awareness. You are aware of reading this book now. You are aware of the words on the page. The conscious mind thinks and plans. You consciously set goals and targets, plan tactics, decide what skills to learn or practice in training. You consciously decide how you are going to take a free kick and where you are going to place it.

The subconscious mind has much, much more depth to it. It contains all your memories, holds your beliefs and values, runs your body functions. Are you aware of your breathing, of your digestion? Who regulates your temperature? And most importantly, your emotions? The subconscious! Using the above free kick example, having decided consciously where you are going to place the free kick, your subconscious takes over by co-ordinating all physical movements which have developed from constant practice.

The goalkeeper receiving your free kick will be unable to react consciously as he has no idea where you are going to place it and as the ball could be travelling at well over 80 mph, will have to react instinctively.

That is why you practice. The subconscious mind will find it difficult to perform a task it has never seen or executed. The better you practice and with constant repetition, the more automatic, competent and smooth you're actions become. When its not possible to physically practice, visualise by using your imagination.

Your subconscious responds to symbolic thought, it sees, hears, feels, tastes and smells. So imagine taking the free kick, see the ball in your minds eye, hear the sound as you kick it and the fans chant your name, feel your foot connecting and smell the freshly cut pitch as you watch the ball head for a top corner of the net

The conscious and subconscious minds can best be described using this analogy. The conscious mind is the team manager, planning tactics, setting targets, analysing the opposition. It's the task of the team – the subconscious, to follow the managers instructions and make his plans happen on the field.

While there is good communication between the manager (conscious mind) and the team (subconscious mind) and the team is well drilled in its duties from training, they should play efficiently. If there is poor communication brought about by low confidence, negative thoughts, poor skills, misunderstanding, then you can imagine what the performance on the field will be like with the manager bellowing uncontrollably from the touch line.

Staying with our free kick example, once you have chosen consciously where to place the ball and you then change your mind as you are about to shoot, you interfere with your body's natural flow, creating poor communication between manager and team, poor communication between conscious and subconscious minds.

That is why practice is so important, especially when working on new tactics or improving specific skills. The more you practice, the more automatic things become for you so you are better able to reproduce them without stopping to think during a game. Remember this, perfect practice makes perfect performance.

Your subconscious mind is like a loyal servant. It wants to serve you, however it needs guidance. It responds best through your senses rather than words. Therefore sights, sounds, feelings, smells and tastes are much more helpful in making your subconscious mind learn what you want it to do.

Lets talk about you …

WHAT ABOUT YOU?

"Be yourself, everyone else is already taken."
OSCAR Wilde

YOUR behaviour is a result of your self-image, the person you believe you really are. Your self-image is so strong, your behaviour will have you perform consistently as the person you think you are.

We all know people who are skilled, yet think they are not. They think they are too fat, too slow, too old, whatever. If you believe that about yourself, if you believe yourself not good enough in any way, you will unconsciously sabotage any effort to make yourself a winner.

Studies have proven time after time, an extraordinary number of sportspeople fail because they think themselves less than they are worth through this limited self-image. Are they unworthy? Of course not. Its how they see themselves in their imagination which affects their performance and may even cause self-destructive behaviour.

Here's an example to prove my point. Sit for a moment somewhere quiet and remember some time in the past when you felt tired, sad, despondent. Really get back into that time by remembering everything you could see and hear in as much detail as you can. Bring back any physical or emotional experiences, get that memory and hold it for a few seconds then try to stand up.

Now sit down again and this time bring back to mind a time when you felt energetic, determined, optimistic. Again remember in as much vivid detail as you can, what you saw, hear the good things that you heard and get in touch with the physical or emotional feelings you had and hold them for several seconds. Now stand up.

Compare the two experiences. In the first you may have found it an effort to stand. How about the second? Did you leap up ready to go? Is it not interesting that in just a few seconds, thinking one way, then another, created an entirely different result. Thoughts influence how you perform. Your belief about yourself influences your thoughts, which affect your behaviour, as this book will prove. I'll discuss the importance of belief more in the next chapter.

That said, let me remind you how quickly a soccer career goes by. For instance, it's incredible how the last twelve months have gone by. How was it for you? Think about your mortality. Imagine your breathing your last. Did you achieve all you wanted to do in soccer? Did you truly live it? Play at the grounds you always wanted? Enjoy wonderful moments with your team mates? Before you know it, you find yourself retired, then into old age and there you are, reflecting on how good you could have been. That is how it ends up for the vast majority of players. Where did all the time go?

The only thing you have total control of in this world is your thinking. At first you may feel self-conscious trying out these methods. Whenever you do something new that takes you beyond your 'comfort zone' you feel nervous. Its ok, your human. You must grit your teeth and get out of your 'comfort zone' and challenge yourself.

This book will open up to you clear ideas as to what you need to do to create the future you want. Nothing in your life is going to change unless you change. You are fully capable of mental and physical feats. You are bigger than you think, capable of more than you can imagine.

You're now in the process of thinking with belief ...

BELIEF

"Man is what he believes."
ANTON Chekhov

YOU are about to take a penalty. You need focus, courage and self-control to outwit an aggressive keeper trying to psych you out. Belief gives you the assurance to trust in you're ability.

Belief dominates behaviour whether positively or negatively and behaviour affects performance. You're physical behaviour is controlled by belief. A belief is knowing with absolute certainty what something means. That belief can mean the difference between an ordinary player and a medal winner. Success or failure – you always prove yourself right. A lower league player can improve and rise in leagues with the desire belief can bring.

Whether you believe you can do something or believe you can't, you're right!

Belief in your ability determines the level of success you will achieve. Once you realise the benefit changing limiting beliefs can do for you, you will have much more motivation to change those limiting beliefs and become a more accomplished player. Performing at, or even near, your true potential, can be as rewarding in itself for some as a winning medal can be for others and one of the reasons why people are happy playing soccer.

In other ways belief can determine your quality of happiness, health, wealth and success. What you believe even has a greater influence on your life than the actual truth.

Notice the successful players. They made more mistakes than those who have not. Every mistake has been accepted as a learning opportunity by them. They continued to believe in themselves. Failure is part of the learning process, not the end of it. Its only a frustration.

Whether you believe you can do something or believe you can not, you're right!

When have you failed? Only when you stop believing. Every response is information to tell you what actions are getting you closer to, or further away from what you want.

We all get stuck in our beliefs, however sensible we think they are. You may find it interesting that you tend to believe what you think is true, without question. If you believe you don't have a good first touch, its because you believe you don't have a good first touch and you will forget any memory of when you performed a good first touch.

But the interesting thing is, if you tell yourself you have, that then gives you permission to question that defeatist belief and soon, with consistent practice, you will find that you have a good first touch – won't you? You will begin to adopt the proper physiology to receive the ball. What you believed is not necessary real, you just need to invest in yourself. Confused? The nice thing about being confused is you come out of it with something new.

Belief creates self-talk, or how you speak to yourself inside your head. I'll discuss that later on. In the meantime, if your going to say something to yourself, you may as well make it something good.

Whether you believe you can do something or believe you can not, you're right!

Take a belief which is holding you back.
Think about or write down its opposite, more positive belief.
Imagine what it would be like living this more positive belief.
Believe that:

You do have the ability to succeed.
You can accomplish anything.
There are no problems, just opportunities.

Your creating your future now.
If you believe your destined to become a successful player, you will be.

Now that kind of thinking can give you a buzz you won't believe!
And the penalty? Assert your authority. Be confident in the face of the goalkeepers hostility and believe the ball is there to be booted into the net!

Whether you believe you can do something or believe you can not, you're right! Am I getting the message across?
Next, believe in the power of imagination …

IMAGINATION

> *"The success I have at free kicks is 5 per cent skill and 95 per cent successful imagery."*
> GIOFRANCO Zola

IMAGINE that I have just cut a lemon in two and I've handed you one of the halves. Notice its texture there in you're hand as you bring it up to your mouth. Be aware of the citric smell while you place the juicy fruit in you're mouth. Now suck on all that tangy lemon juice and let it run down you're throat.

As you are reading this, imagine you have submerged both in a bucket of hot, soapy water. You can remember what that is like? Did you have a bath last night, wash the windows, even your car? Recall that feeling of hot soapy water on your hands, make it vivid, feel those pinpricks of watery heat.

Your subconscious mind can not tell the difference between a real, or imagined event, it's just like a DVD recorder! It records sights and sounds continuously. Your body then treats every vivid thought and image as if it was real. Ever awakened from a nightmare? Notice how your body responds to the vivid use of you're imagination more so than a conscious command. If you order your heart to speed up, it probably will not. If you imagine in detail walking down a sinister dark alley, late at night and hear fast, approaching footsteps behind you, I bet you're heartbeat will increase. What about that nightmare? It wasn't real but you woke up in a sweat, you're heart pounding, gripped with fear and it took a while for you to calm down.

Some people claim they cannot visualise as they don't see in pictures clearly. That's ok, just have a sense of a picture in your mind. It does not have to be as clear as your vision is while reading this book. Everyone has the ability to imagine, I may have just proven it to you. If not, answer these questions:

Think of your locker in your changing room. What does it look like? Where is the door handle? What sound does it make when you shut it? To answer, you had to use you're imagination.

Now by changing the pictures and sounds of the mind, you can gain conscious control of any aspect of you're game. Image's that are bigger, brighter, bolder have a greater impact than those which are smaller, duller and further away. Let me show you.

Think of someone you found stressful to play against or who rankled you. Think about facing them again. Notice how the bad memory of them can hurt you like a knife. They can beat you without a ball being kicked. Here's something your going to love. Recall their face. As you do so, ask yourself:

Is the memory in black and white or in colour?
Is their face in your memory to the left, to the right, or there right in front of you?
Is the face large or small?
Is it light or dark? Moving or still?
Are there any sounds?

Now play around with the way you remember that person. Make each of these changes in turn and notice what happens:

If the memory has colour, drain it all away until it is like a black and white photo.
Move the position of the face and push it further away from you. Shrink it down in size.
Turn down the brightness, make it fuzzy.
If the image is moving, freeze frame it, if still, animate it.

What sound do you hear? Is it their voice? Change it by giving them a squeaky voice like a cartoon character, or a deep sexy one, go on, do it.
Finally, give the face a clown's nose, bright coloured hair, Mickey Mouse ears. Go on, have fun!

Altering your memory can change how you feel. Think of that person again in this new way. How do you feel about them now? Probably the stressful memory had diminished if not gone completely. Not only do you feel different now, imagine how much more comfortable you will feel the next time you face that person. It's your control, your emotion, your thinking that belongs to you, not someone else controlling you.

***

Mental training through visualisation is an essential tool in the soccer players arsenal. Professionals understand the importance of rehearsing skills often in their minds. They become so well prepared, they are able to go onto 'autopilot' when they need to use those skills for real. Most soccer activities are done subconsciously. Do you deliberately think about the actions of taking a throw in? Taking a free kick? Jumping to head the ball? Of course not, you do it naturally.

Here's how you can imagine playing a whole game? If you visualised the whole game at normal speed it would become tiresome. You know the key events that affect you throughout the game, so speed up the game in general and when you come to the parts which involve you, bring it back to normal speed.

Visualising different scenarios helps prepare you for any eventuality during a game. But reality is not always as perfect as you would like to imagine. One key to successful visualisation is dealing with unforeseen challenges and problems that happen before, during and after a game. Make a list of things that could go wrong and then practice overcoming them and you will be better prepared for all possibilities. Regardless of what problem you have happen during the game, imagine it turning out right for you.

***

Let me show you how to use imagination in a way known as association and dissociation. This is where visualisation skills really pay off. Association means re-living the event as if it is really happening, seeing through your own eyes, hearing the sounds and feeling all the feelings. Dissociation is noticing the situation as if you are watching yourself in a movie. As you are more detached from the action, there is less emotional impact.

Think of a stressful or uncomfortable memory, maybe a bad game. How did you feel? Keep that image in your mind. Now step out of yourself so you can see the back of your head. I know you may be sceptical, at least give me a hearing. Now move as far away from that situation you are remembering as you can. Step all the way out of the picture so you can still see it, but way over there somewhere as if its happening to someone else. Shrink it down. Lose all the colour. Turn the background fuzzy or white. Fade away any sound. Notice by dissociating reduces the intensity of the feelings you were having. Do those emotions feel less now? It takes courage to learn new skills such as these.

You can do the same to heighten a good memory, by association. When you think about happy memories, you re-create the happy feelings associated with them. Remember a game when you felt really confident, aware of your ability, strength and self-belief. Now let the image come into you're mind. Make it juicy. Step into that memory as if you were there again, seeing through you're own eyes, hearing through you're own ears and feeling how successful you felt in your body. Enlarge the memory, make it bigger and brighter, the feelings stronger, turn up the sounds, make everything richer. If you can not remember a time, imagine how it would feel to be totally confident – you get what you focus on.

There you have it. To reduce a negative memory, step out, move away from it (dissociate). Watch it as if its happening to someone else, shrink it, turn it black and white, dull, out of focus. Make the sounds quieter, further away. Doing this can cause any bad emotional response to drain away. Notice your controlling how it affects you.

And to improve a positive memory, zoom in and fully experience it (associate). Make the image bigger and closer, intensify the colours, increase the brightness, make the sounds closer and louder, unless it's a memory of peace and quiet. Live it. You can have a great deal of fun with these methods.

***

Here's an experiment. Players in other positions can adapt this for themselves. You're a striker and for some reason you have lost the greed and the goals have dried up. Psychologically its becoming an issue as you keep re-running those missed scoring chances in your mind.

First visualise yourself sat in the dug out (associated) during a past game watching yourself on the field (dissociated). What encouragement and advice would you give that 'you' who is playing? Let that mental film run while you watch yourself and stop the film at a point when 'you' missed a goal scoring chance. Being dissociated, this should help you remember the moment but without the negative emotional content.

Freeze frame that image. Here is where you get to have fun. Play with the image. If its in colour, drain it away and turn it to black and white. If its vivid, de-focus it. Change any sounds and their location. Change any feelings.

Rewind. Start the movie again in all its glory. This time associate in, make everything real and speed it all up until you reach the point just before 'you' failed to score. Now you are associated, play the film at normal speed and adjust everything so it turns the missed scoring chance into a goal. Speed it all up again as you send the ball flying into the net.

After celebrating the goal with your team mates and feeling how good you will feel, dissociate from the pitch and go back to the dug out. Associate in and applaud you're goal scorer, give useful feedback and repeat that visualisation several times until it begins to feel like a real memory.

***

Imagine you are defending. Step into a picture of yourself controlling the ball, tackling, volleying, clearing and heading almost at will. Feel mighty and proud. Hear the 'thud' of every perfectly hit ball. Notice the opponents. Forwards, midfielders. Shrink them down and turn them into black and white, move them further away from you, duller, quieter. None of them able to make any penetration. Now do the same yourself, this time as a forward – go on, I'm not going to do everything for you!

***

You can use your imagination to free yourself from any old, negative beliefs that might be limiting you. That's right! Imagine they are written or painted on a wall. With a ball at your feet, boot it at the wall so you demolish the wall completely See the dust, hear the bricks tumbling down, feel the energy you are using until those negative words or image are totally destroyed.

You could imagine them drawn or written on paper. Feel the paper between your hands as you rip it to shreds, hear it, feel it, see it happen there in you're minds eye. Finish off by ritually burning it. I said some methods would challenge you – this is all revolutionary stuff!

Here's an easier one. Close your eyes and imagine in your mind a picture of the player you wish to become. See yourself in your kit, you're balanced stance, the expression on your face, all the tiny details. Take that picture and throw it up into the air and multiply it so that hundreds of copies come raining down all around you as far as the eye can see. They even go into you're past and future.

Did that feel awkward? Exercises like these may seem silly at first, but while you control the pictures in you're mind and how they sound, you are not at the mercy of anyone else or circumstance and they direct you're subconscious mind toward being the soccer player you want to be. A flame will ignite inside you.

Maybe imagine once or twice not doing as well so you can bring all your emotions into it. Do not just visualise the best-case scenarios. Be prepared with a plan B and also a plan C. Do not imagine failing, but mentally plan how you will respond to unpleasant or difficult situations. This happens sooner or later when games do not go exactly as hoped. You can still be proud of putting 100% effort in.

I'll teach you next about self-talk ...

SELF-TALK

"My life has been full of terrible misfortunes, most of which never happened."
MICHEL de Montaigne

ALSO known as internal dialogue, self-talk is simply the way you talk to yourself inside you're head. You worry over a bad pass, congratulate yourself after a good result, even tell yourself how sexy you look in your fresh, clean, kit. People do it everyday, but mostly it's negative. Blaming yourself, chastising yourself. "I'm not good enough," "I'm too tired," "I'm too old." This is one of the major causes of poor performance. If you tell yourself something often enough, you will begin to believe it. It may not be true, but you will certainly believe it is. If you have negative beliefs, you have negative self-talk which will confirm the negative belief and so it goes on.

You must be aware of your internal dialogue. While positive thinking may not always work, negative thinking almost always does. Put aside any self-pity and accept the responsibility to change. If the voice you use is not supporting you, change it.

A major problem for sport people is repeated dwelling over poor performance. This memory leads to negative self-talk along with emotional discomfort. A pessimistic mind may then remember similar bad events. Allowing the past to affect you instead of focusing on the present only slows you down. You suffer tight muscles, energy loss, poor coordination, which all add to the bad performance. Future chapters will cover techniques to get you over these poor memories.

Be good to yourself when you talk to yourself by talking positively. Make mental pictures of yourself being a total success. See yourself winning, hear the congratulations of you're team mates, the applause of the spectators and feel how good you feel when you practice being a winner. Mental rehearsal is the next best thing to actually being successful, so do it as often as you can and review it with positive self-talk. You will be delighted when you witness your future.

What do you say to yourself when things go wrong?
What do you say to yourself when confronted by a challenge?

The secret is confident players will talk differently to themselves than those who lack confidence, even though they perform equally well. Playing with confidence gives you the security to enjoy every minute and will be reflected in you're game. Without that confidence, another player may always feel unprepared, nervous, undecided. Those thoughts will then reinforce those beliefs. So you see how vital confident, positive self-talk is.

Self-talk after a good performance:

Confident player	**Player lacking confidence**
I am like that.	It was luck.
I always perform like that.	It was a one-off.
I'll be the same next time.	I can't do that again.

Self-talk after a poor performance:

Confident player	**Player lacking confidence**
It was luck.	I am like that.
It was a one-off.	I always perform like that.
I can't do that again.	I'll be the same next time.

Keep track of the positive or negative thoughts you have about yourself so you can change any negative thinking to a more positive outlook. Making positive affirmations (self-talk) will help you feel more confident, but to work effectively, these affirmations need to be inspiring and practical. Boastful declarations such as "I'm the best player in the league" or "nobody can tackle like me" become banana skins as they do not work in the real world and you will end up looking foolish, so take care.

You will find affirmations such as "I am prepared and ready to defend" repeated slowly and thoughtfully can lead to calmness. This gives you a positive mindset and leads to clear thinking and good judgement.

Are you holding yourself back through perfectionism …

PERFECTIONISM

"I don't care what you say about me, just spell my name right!"
P. T. Barnum

A perfectionist can get hung up doing things perfectly. They can be their own worst enemy because they are never satisfied with their performance. A self-critical perfectionist can never be perfect in their own mind because of a fear of making mistakes. That is the greatest barrier to success. Beneath the desire to succeed and reach excellence, a perfectionist often has an ultra-negative, condemning voice going on inside their head.

Yes, a perfectionist hates to lose, but a perfectionist must not get anxious about losing.

For some perfectionists, their belief is anything less than perfect is unacceptable. Even when they are playing well they are unable to feel any real fulfilment, as in their eyes, they never do anything of sufficient high standard to warrant feelings of satisfaction.

Striving to be too perfect can create failure. Even when they are playing well, perfectionists have trouble feeling good about themselves. Fear of losing, making mistakes, the need for control, obsessive or unrealistic expectation all causes anxiety, misery, dissatisfaction. Team mates and family can be offended as the perfectionist can be as critical of others as they are of themselves.

Perfectionism does create positive qualities. An ambitious drive to succeed, an inclination to plan and organise and a focus on developing excellence. These people can be highly effective and energetic.

But perfectionists easily become discouraged by failing to meet the impossible aspirations they set for themselves. Inefficiency, inconsistency, delays and poor results can create a reluctance to take on new challenges, so they accomplish less rather then adjust their ambitions more realistically. Anxiety, indecision and low self-esteem may become a result.

With a fear of failure and criticism, perfectionists avoid opportunities to take chances and do not sometimes develop their skill further. They may postpone important tasks if situations are not in their favour if the time or situation is not suitable for them. They will procrastinate until they can look good.

Some psychologists believe perfectionists are that way due to conditional parenting. The child's role in life has already been decided. Rarely satisfied parents who want their offspring to be a sporting success have no idea what they are doing to their child's self-esteem with their critical comments. When they criticise, they are telling their child, or so the child believes, s/he is a failure in their parents eyes. Children are easily influenced and will develop that fear of failure, affecting them unconsciously for years to come.

On the other hand, children coming from a volatile, neglected family life may think doing everything to perfection will get them reward, recognition and help them apply some control over their unstable environment.

Do you set high standards for your performance?
Do you feel frustrated if you cannot meet your goals?
Is your best never good enough for you?
Do you worry about never measuring up to your ambitions?
Do you believe dwelling on mistakes is important?

So, when you do well do you give yourself enough credit? When you do poorly do you verbally beat yourself up? Do you punish yourself if you make a mistake and gang up on yourself. All soccer players experience failure at some stage, its how you emotionally handle it that determines if you leave it in the past or re-create it over and over.

You are human. Perfectionism damages excellence. Perfectionism does not exist, excellence does. Focus on the things you can control.

Put errors behind you, loosen the stays on your self-criticism – let it go! Don't get angry with yourself, move on. Concentrate on the next ball, on what is happening right in front of you, in the present. Forget what's just happened, its history. You don't have to be perfect at every aspect of soccer and besides, team mates, family, friends might like you more if you have some frailties.

A perfect footballer is optimistic, do you think he will criticise himself ...

THE INNER CRITIC

"We don't see things as they are, but rather as we are."
ANAIS Nin

EVERYBODY is a critic and the worst one you will ever come across is the one inside your head. This kind of talk has a detrimental effect on your emotional state, even worse than someone in the crowd screaming at you. What does it sound like? Is it angry, sarcastic, resigned? When you make a mistake I bet you never say "good, that's another learning experience."

People think because there is a voice inside their head, they must listen to it. You can choose.

It is important to analyse what you do in soccer, but only relative to the situation. Criticism should be constructive feedback if its going to be of any use. If critical self-talk is not supporting you, play with the direction and tone of the voice. Like many of the methods presented in this book, this one may seem strange at first. Go give it a shot, you have nothing to lose and everything to gain if it works for you. Is that reasonable?

Your team's behind, the clocks ticking down, you berate yourself for uncertain footwork.

Notice your critical voice and its nasty tone.

Now notice where it is coming from. Inside or outside your head? From the front, side, back?

If you're right-handed, extend your left arm, left handed, extend your right.
Stick up the thumb of the extended arm.
Wherever the critical voice came from, imagine you can move it away from your head to your shoulder, then to your elbow, on to your wrist, now move it all the way down to the very tip of your thumb.
Hear the voice repeat the same thing, only this time as if you hear the voice coming from the tip of your thumb. Slow it right down, or speed it up. Change it to be like Mickey Mouse, or another cartoon character. Change the tone to something comical.
Move the voice all the way down to your big toe.
You can even use another voice to make the negative one shut up.

This technique can also be used on bad memories of someone talking critically to you. You can understand this, can you not?

I'll make an interesting comment about critical self-talk. It always takes a hold in the subconscious as a command. So if you tell yourself your going to take a bad corner kick, lose a tackle, shoot wide, then it will probably happen. This is because negative self-talk generally has a strong emotion attached to it. A positive suggestion, no matter how good the intention, is usually taken as wishful thinking, so it does not contain the emotional content.

If you want to change for the better, pay close attention to the words you use on yourself, they can change the way you perform. They are that magical. And when you repeat something with enough exciting emotion, you start to believe it. Use words and phrases that will motivate you and fill you with enthusiasm for the game. Every sportsperson has two competing voices going on inside their head, one is a negative critic, the other a positive coach. Who you listen to is your choice.

Let's re-programme your self-image …

Re-programme Your Self-Image

"We are never deceived; we deceive ourselves."
GOETHE

USING conscious logical thinking, you know the required response you want to a game situation. But its not you're logical mind that manages the response, its you're subconscious which controls heart rate, breathing, perspiration as well as the emotions of pride, resentment, fear or desire.

To alter any poor memories or attitudes you may have about you're game, first weaken them, then create better alternatives by using the methods outlined in this book. You will be able to go into activities and situations with an abundance of enthusiasm. Just give yourself time.

Clasp your hands in your usual way, fingers entwined and notice which thumb is on top. Let go then clasp your hands again in such a way as the opposite thumb is on top. How does it feel? Awkward? Uncomfortable? It doesn't feel natural! This shows the further you go into unfamiliar territory, the greater the psychological discomfort. Your performance may suffer temporarily as you make needed adjustments to your game, but change does that. If you were to place your hands and thumb the 'awkward' way every time, it would eventually feel natural, as your skill adjustments will.

You have talent. Can you adjust to a new squad or league? This method will show how you can perform with confidence:
Take a deep breath, sit back and relax as you exhale.
Tighten, then relax all your muscle groups.
Recall the sights, sounds, feelings of you playing at your very best.
In your minds eye imagine another you standing in front of you. This is the best that you have ever been, or ever will be, at the top of your game, every decision you make is the right one.
If you can't see it or imagine it, just know that it is there.
When you feel happy with the image in front of you, notice the way you stand, move, kick, pass, trap, head.
Notice a confident champion before you, spreading out accurate passes every time, an unstoppable outfielder or unbeatable goalkeeper.
Now step into your image and see through those eyes, hear through those ears and feel how good it feels to be that living image.
Keep that important feeling and make everything bigger, brighter, more powerful. Let it glow.
Step into another more intense image of yourself. Keep doing it several times more, getting bigger and brighter and stronger each time.
Take a few minutes if you wish to imagine yourself in any situation from the past where you want a bad memory changed to a more positive outcome, or see yourself in a future situation dominating play, being rewarded, excelling. You can, you know, forget about ever having had that problem.
Daydream and know it can come true.
Think of a future situation or event when having a positive feeling is desired. Taking a direct free kick for example. You have read the routine above, give it a go, or try this one next:

***

Using the Circle of Excellence exercise builds a positive mood and creates a state of mind which will be useful in the future.
In front of you, create the Circle of Excellence. This represents that state you require. Imagine it has a colour, maybe there is also a sound there, or a special word. This circle brings for you all the skills and positive assurance you want.

Now, return to a time when you had that positive resource, or imagine you had the right attitude, dedication and grit.
Take a deep breath, exhale ...
Step inside the circle.
As you enter, imagine the bright colour shinning down and all around you, going into every cell of your body, from the top of your head, all the way down to the tip of your toes. Double the brightness. Hear the special sound or word. Imagine that feeling you have getting stronger, being absorbed by your body. Feel the strength and enthusiasm that glows from you.
Tell yourself you are more confident, talented, fitter.
Every breath you take, you take in more of the resource, your demoralising the opposition, everything you do is a bonus to the team. If you can see it in your minds eye, you can achieve it.

You can do the Circle of Excellence just about everywhere. Rehearse it first, then going onto the pitch imagine the circle before you as you cross the touch line. Do it as you take position for a set piece. How about stepping out of the shower, getting out of a car.

Feeling good? You're learning to master your emotions ...

MASTER YOUR EMOTIONS

"No matter how thin you slice it, there are always two sides."
BARUCH Spinoza

YOU keep coming back for more now, don't you. Any unpleasant thought you have comes with an unpleasant feeling. If you want to win the game going on inside your head, you have to deal with emotions. I'm going to guide you to be you're most confident self and feel resourceful in just a moment, for any endeavour you choose.

You will come across a broad range of emotions naturally during a match which may predict the performance you are going to have. By being aware and monitoring your emotions you can become aware of you're optimal performance state.

You may be wondering what is an emotion? An emotion is the mood you are in at any particular moment and is individual and unique to all of us. Love, hate, confidence, fear, they are all emotions and we constantly go in and out of them all day long. All behaviour is the result of an emotion.

Remember times when you were filled with confidence, determination, joy, optimism. Unfortunately, you also suffered anger, resentment and regret. Emotions are your subconscious minds way of telling you there is something going on you should pay attention too.

***

Here, you'll learn how to programme yourself to experience more of the resourceful emotions you want in all the situations you want. The pictures you make inside your imagination and the way you talk to yourself are known as internal representations. And that is all they are, representations, not real life, so they cannot harm you.

Changes in breathing, muscle tension, posture, even facial expression all influence you're feelings and behaviour, as you may now begin to appreciate.

Think of a time when you felt nervous, anxious, deflated. Notice how it affects your posture, your shoulders slump down and your head may have dropped.

I can show you a simple way to change. Wherever you are, plant your feet firmly on the ground, hold yourself tall, pull those shoulders back, take a great big breath, let it out, look up at the ceiling or the sky and put a great big grin on your face. Smile with your whole face with feeling. Now try to remember that bad situation again. Notice your mood has probably lifted and you no longer remember it in the same unpleasant way.

Why not keep the feeling there. Stand straight, let your spine support you while you imagine a bright golden thread running up your spine and straight out to the sky. Let yourself relax, held up by this golden thread.

If your body is tense, it is producing different chemicals to when it is relaxed, so you feel and think differently. See how making physiological changes makes a difference to your emotional response.

And there's a lot said about Anchoring ...

ANCHORING

"Don't find fault, find a remedy."
HENRY Ford

REMEMBER how you can use 'The Circle of Excellence' to bring about a resourceful state? So with anchoring. Its like having a 'push button' to feel excellence.

If you, or one of your players, is feeling anxious about a forthcoming game and want to look forward to the game positive, you can add resources of confidence, concentration, relaxation or excitement by applying a resource anchor. The theory behind resource anchors is if you constantly link the mood or emotion you desire to be in with a meaningful feeling, sight, sound, or even a taste or smell, you can reproduce that desired mood or emotion when you need it.

Anchors exist all around you. Have you come across an old photo which created a pang of nostalgia? Heard an old song which was popular during a special time in your life? Smelt a particular aroma that brought memories rushing back? Do you frequently visit a location and always feel compelled to sit at the same place? Hold a new born baby and notice how your emotional state changes.

All these associations trigger memories that take us back to a past experience. They are called anchors as they 'anchor' you to a certain emotional state. The clever thing is you can use these anchors to bring back a whole positive experience.

Setting up an anchor only takes a few minutes. Read the routine a couple of times to get it clear in your head. Create a physical signal which you are going to use. What you read in many NLP books is to touch you're thumb and forefinger together, but it can be any appropriate signal, patting down your hair, scratching an imaginary itch, clasping you're hands a certain way, rubbing a wrist, making a fist, its all up to you. Even repeating a phrase or word may do the trick for you.

Now, vividly remember a time when you had the ability or emotion you want to repeat. Add as much detail as you can. As you rewind the clock, see what you saw, hear what you heard, feel how you felt then. Relive it in all its glory. Now see, hear, feel even more, fully experience it intensely. Let it all come back to you. Let it build up so you relive it in your whole body. If you can't remember a time, imagine how you would feel if you had the confidence, success or joy.

As the memory 'peaks' fire the physical signal you designed. Sink into the feeling of really being there again, make it brighter, richer, turn up the volume.

Now break state by doing something like remembering a friends telephone number, saying you're name backwards, or remembering a nursery rhyme as a distraction, so when you repeat this technique, its like doing it afresh.

Get back into the memory and allow it to 'peak' again. Repeat four or five times. You can bring in different, positive memories if you wish, rather than staying with the same one. You choose. Remember to break state each time.

Test to see if the anchor works. Break state by thinking of something else. Then fire the anchor to test if you can trigger the response you want. You should get back the resourceful state. If not, apply the stimulus several more times and test again.

There is usually a couple of good reasons if you are having trouble. Make sure you are actually reliving the event rather than just thinking about it. You must be able to feel the positive resource. Have one specific resource in mind to anchor rather than getting confused juggling several.

This gets better. Whenever you feel you are experiencing that resource as you go about you're normal life, anchor it with the same stimulus you devised so you are 'topping up.'

The great think with using anchors is they work automatically. Think about a forthcoming event when you will require a particular feeling or emotion. Imagine everything going perfectly. Picture it in your mind, seeing, hearing, feeling yourself in this good state at that future time. Now fire your anchor.

By following those steps you can create very resourceful states for yourself or your players. If working with someone, its best for you to also be in the same resourceful state as the player wants. If any states, or emotions your player want seem to be in conflict, being motivated but relaxed for example, ask that person if they feel they can be in both states at the same time. If they believe they can, all well and good. If not, it's best to create two different anchors, one for relaxed and another for motivated which you apply separately.

Practice anchoring to place yourself into more resourceful states. Do it when you are in different positions or environments. Go to different locations and practice getting yourself into positive moods. You can look back with satisfaction to see how much further you have developed.

***

You now understand how you can become 'anchored' to certain states, unfortunately, just as there are resourceful anchors in your life that can bring you good feelings, you may also realise how you can create negative states. Playing at a venue with negative memories for you, or against a defender or forward who has had the better of you in the past, can make you feel helpless and powerless. You may have negative anchors and they can be disconnected by a process called 'collapsing anchors.'

Unless you're a coach applying this with one of your players, its best to have someone go through this process with you, as you will need their help to fix the anchors in place. Ensure you understand the method thoroughly and you feel comfortable with it before you work with anyone.

If working with a player, explain the process and what the player can achieve from it. Be in full agreement that the negative state is to be collapsed and decide what resourceful state is going to replace it. Make sure you are replacing a negative state with a very strong, positive one.

Decide where you are going to apply the resource and remove the negative state from. To keep things simple, you would apply the resource stimulus to one side of the body, be it the right knuckles, right shoulder, right knee and remove the negative state from the left knuckles, left shoulder, or left knee.

Fully remember an unwanted state or memory. For example lets say 'apprehensive.' Re-live it and feel the emotion kicking in. On a scale of 0 – 10 how do you or the players feel about the situation? Anchor it kinesthetically somewhere on the body, say for example, squeezing the left knee. Only do this once. Break state then test the anchor works by squeezing the left knee.

Break state by thinking of something else. This is important.

Now, access fully a positive state or memory you have experienced, lets go for 'capable' and anchor that kinaesthetically somewhere else, this time lets say squeezing the right knee. Repeat the whole positive state process several times, then test the anchor works by squeezing the right knee.

Fully relive, or have the player fully relive the event intensely and as the good feelings 'peak' they should give you a pre-arranged signal, a nod of the head for example so you can then anchor the positive resource into position.

Break state again.

Now here's the good bit. Fire both anchors by squeezing both knees simultaneously and then let go of the left knee while continuing to hold onto the right knee for about five seconds longer. Watch the players reaction. S/he should go through a series of emotions for a few seconds until that resourceful state is fixed. As long as the resourceful states anchor is stronger than the undesired states, the undesired anchor will collapse and the un-resourceful state will no longer affect you or them. If you picked a strong negative memory, you may need more positive resources to make the situation more satisfying.

Test by asking on a scale of 0 – 10 how do you or your player now feel about the issue which was bothering them.

Future pace by imagining yourself or asking the player to imagine some time in the future when they would face that situation again and notice the response. If the problem has gone, continue imagining *facing the old problem at a number of future events weeks, months, or even years ahead until both you, or the player, are certain the problem has gone.*

Next we can talk about Pressure ...

Pressure

"When you have fun, it changes all the pressure into pleasure."
KEN Griffeyn

PRESSURE gets a bad name. It's the ultimate lie detector. When its present it can be a positive force bringing out the best in you, or a negative one, being an excuse to quit. Some soccer players break through, while those less committed break down. Everyone feels pressure in big games, no one is immune. It can often start long before the game begins. Soccer players under pressure become internally self-conscious rather then externally task-conscious. Worrying about making a mistake will usually get them one.

Recall a time when you felt pressure. Remember what you were doing, feeling, saying. Where you excited or nervous? Did you expect failure or feel a desire to win? Did you let all kinds of negative thoughts come into your mind?

Excessive mental pressure often produces mental blocks. Then anything recently learnt in training, be it technical or tactical may well be confusing or forgotten. Some situations can be embarrassing or humiliating, especially in front of team mates or supporters. These experiences lodge themselves in the mind and body, showing up as performance problems either right away, or lying dormant for days, weeks or months before raising their ugly heads.

Demands on players are higher than ever the higher up the leagues you go. Sponsorship, TV, money, fans all increase the pressure. Become mentally tough, look at pressure as a challenge to drive yourself that much more harder.

Pressure creates muscle tension, causing over-tightness, generally in the neck and shoulders. The heart beat goes up, breathing quickens, skin perspires. Some players feel their stomach churn. A tense, stressed out player will kick the ball with a tense, stressed out foot.

When you are tense, you want to get any task over as soon as possible. Mentally you're mind races. The more you hurry, the worse you will probably play, making mistakes, creating even more pressure and greater muscle tension, so wasting more energy. Consider this, stress is internal. Stress does not exist outside of you're mind. Soccer challenges do not become anxious, only players do.

One effective method is simply to write down you're specific stressors. The simple act of recording a behaviour you wish to change leads to improvements in the required direction.

Interestingly, a way to relax tense muscles is first tighten them further. If you're shoulders feel like coiled springs, slowly draw them up and squeeze them. Hold for 15 seconds. Feel the sensation. Then release slowly and relax completely. Notice how they feel.

Use travel time to listen to inspirational audiotapes or CD's. Hearing someone you admire and respect can have a positive impact on you're mood. Upbeat music can make the miles fly by or maybe something soothing to keep you calm en-route.

Stop reading this chapter right now and do the following breathing exercise. Close your eyes and take a deep breath down into your abdomen. Count to three as you inhale through your nose and count to five as you exhale through your mouth. Do that five times. Notice if you pay attention to your breathing and the counting, you should after five breaths, begin to feel more relaxed.

You can even enhance that deep breathing technique by remembering a time when you were on top of you're game. As you breath in and focus on the picture, say to yourself a word or phrase that can represent the relaxed feeling. "Steady" or "easy" might do. Play around and notice what works for you.

You can do this anytime. Think about your best long passes, tackles, goals scored, goal line clearances, penalty saves. All past achievements and successes from using your skills and the good feelings they created. Stop any negative thinking as soon as you are aware of any and use you're imagination to think about you're strengths and resources. Make them all bigger and brighter and louder. Remember good moods and things that make you smile.

Days before an important game, or a trial, a little nervousness may creep in. So actually the game begins before the game begins. At home, the journey to the venue, in the changing room. How do you reduce pressure and place you're mind in the here and now? Here's one method to give yourself an advantage. When you arrive in the changing room, use each article of clothing you remove, jacket, shirt, trousers, one shoe, then the other, to let go of a concern or irrational fear.

Each article of kit you put on, imagine you are putting on resources of energy, courage or resilience. By the time you have changed, any distraction you were focused on will have dissolved. Now you are in the right time zone and in the best state of mind for what is ahead.

Lets see how you can drive away the spectre of anger ...

ANGER & PSYCHING

"Learn to control your emotions or they will control you."
EDGAR Martinez

SOCCER is an emotional sport and when anger raises its ugly head, you must be able to deal with it. Anger is born out of frustration and expectation. It feeds on itself. When you allow anger to get the best of you, it generally brings out the worst in you. Anger blocks concentration, tactics and technique. Your Temper can hurt your team mates. Too many red cards and they will find it difficult to trust you and you may despise yourself for being so self-destructive.

You can allow opponents or situations to tie you up in knots. Your heart beats faster, your breathing quickens. So, you are stood there, all clenched jaw, bulging eyes and hunched up shoulders, hacked off and out of control. At the extreme, you do not notice other people, you do not notice you're surroundings and you do not do anything sensible. Or you can learn from it.

You control you're mood and emotions. If someone makes you angry, you are giving that person power over you. They are then controlling you're moods and emotions.

Anger can often be fear in disguise, as anger is based on insecurity and a need to protect yourself. Non-violent fighting spirit is based on self-confidence. Have you noticed, anger only has a temporary boosting effect which produces unreliable results. Once it has been released, sadness, regret or remorse usually follow.

Players who cannot control their anger will never make great players. The best have the maturity to master their emotions, not to be servants to them. That emotional energy allows you to raise you're game. Many sportspeople can channel anger positively in this way as it motivates them. Anger kept under control will work for you.

You cannot have a blind rage of anger if you remain calm. If you have an anger button, there is something you can do about it. While you are reading this, get yourself relaxed as we are going to set a calm button as a resource before another anger moment arises. For convenience, we will set the 'anchors' to your waist so you could do this while you are standing when the ball goes out of play. Being inconspicuous, nobody will have a clue what you are doing. But you can set it anywhere that is convenient for you.

Close eye's and think of a recent game situation when you lost your cool, or think about things that may trigger anger for you on a regular basis. Now, just for a moment, really get back into it, get fully immersed into that experience, see everything, hear what you heard, feel exactly the way you felt.

Now step out of the experience as if you are watching someone else and rewind the scene as if you were rewinding a video until you reach the very first moment that anger began to develop. Go back a couple more frames or a few seconds, whichever feels right for you and imagine a large red button and anchor that somewhere on your body, we'll say on your left waist.

Open your eye's and say your name backward or remember a friends telephone number to break state, then close eyes again.

Now take three deep breaths, exhaling out for longer than the in-breath. Think of a relaxing time, a good holiday, being on a beach, a quiet walk beside a lake, or a funny moment. Something that makes you smile on the outside as well as the inside. Really relax and get into the moment.

Where do you feel that feeling? Let it spread throughout you're body, going to the top of your head and all the way down to the tips of you're toes. See it as a colour, feel it as a great feeling, or hear it as a sound.

As it begins to 'peak' imagine a big green button on the right waist. Press this several times and let the good feelings amplify.

Open your eyes. Say you're name backward. Now, press your red button and immediately after, your green button and hold them both

for a moment before releasing the red button while continuing to hold the green a bit longer.
Repeat the sequence another half dozen times until triggering the green button automatically creates a calm response.

***

Psyching or gamesmanship comes with the territory. Cheating, provocation, verbal abuse, lie's are all designed to upset you emotionally and disrupt concentration. Recognise it for what it is and do not allow it to get inside you're head and ruin you're composure. If it affects you, its there, at the back of your mind. Even if you pretend it does not bother you, it does.

Be also aware there are two kinds of psyching – one the opposition does and the one you do to yourself. Come closer my friend. A way to divert anger is to divert your attention. Develop a ritual when you need to calm yourself or when you need a few moments to get yourself together. Pick a spot or a mark on the field or around the ground, a line or a corner flag for example. When the ball goes out of play, walk to the mark and touch it, or if that is not possible, look at it. This strategy can help keep your mind focused while you give yourself a pep talk.

Do not get annoyed with the referee even if he is as blind as a bat. Accept any decision and get on with the game, he will not change his mind. Everything evens out in the end.

You only need one or two simple reminders to stay in control. Do something physical to slow events down for yourself. Rub you're hands together, tie you're boot laces, touch a goal post, nothing too complicated. These are all small psychological boosts for mental and emotional management. At half-time, change into fresh dry kit, even change your boots or put on a sweat band. Do some small change to make things feel like it's a new start.

You could always do onto others what they do to you. Often they dish it out, but cannot take it. You are now taking the initiative. However, do you really need to lower yourself to their level. The best response is be mature and have compassion for someone who has to resort to gamesmanship to defeat you as they cannot do it through talent alone. By the way, humour can be a great weapon.

Lets calm ourselves with breathing …

BREATHING

"They can because they think they can."
VIRGIL

OFTEN overlooked, breathing is essential to life but do you realise, correct breathing is essential to good performance and should be carried out at all times. Then, your body is subconsciously maintaining the balance of oxygen and carbon dioxide. When you feel tense, apprehensive, breathing changes to a shallow, fast breathing which will adversely affect you're physiology as it causes dizziness, poor vision, tiredness or breathlessness which will only increase further anxiety.

If you practice correct breathing, it becomes second nature, so you must breath properly when you are anxious, as it will help keep you 'grounded.' There are three features to breathing, first the rate or how fast or slow, second is location, be it clavicular, chest, or abdomen and lastly where you inhale and exhale, through your mouth or nose.

High or clavicular breathers fill only the upper portion of their lungs, so only a small amount of air can enter. Stale air remains in the bottom portion of their lungs and impurities are not properly eliminated. These people always seem to be gulping or gasping for breath.

Most people breath into the chest area as mid or intercostals breathers. This is still not efficient as their chest is only partially expanded.

Low or abdominal breathing is the best way as it takes in reasonable quantities of air and expels impurities from the lungs.

Where do you breath?

Lie on your back. Place one hand on your chest and the other on your abdomen. Breath out to empty your lungs. Now breath in your normal fashion. Do not force it as you may get light-headed in which case give it a rest till you feel better.

As you breath, which hand rises and falls the most? If it's the one on your chest, well, you are not breathing deeply enough. You should be breathing into your abdomen.

Here's how. Imagine a position an inch or two below your naval and you are sending the breath you breath, down to it. You should feel your stomach area swell as you inhale. If it does not, place something light, like a paperback book on your abdomen and as you inhale through your nose, concentrate on making it rise.

When you breath into the chest, usually you are only filling those lungs about three-quarters full, the bottom quarter remaining stale air. Breathing into the abdomen actually fills the bottom of your lungs with fresh, rich air which can only do you good.

Here's another trick. As you inhale into your abdomen and feel it expand, pull back your shoulders and your head while you inhale some more, this will fill the top of your lungs.

Oxygen is energy. It helps relax the muscles and clears the mind. When you hold your breath, maybe when taking a penalty, you create pressure and a nervous feeling develops. Slow, deep breathing will make you feel relaxed, improve the quality of your blood, gives you better health, keeping your body and mind in the present.

When you look at the mechanics of breathing you realise that breathing in, or holding your breath the moment you perform an exertion instead of exhaling, is completely wrong. It places your body under more strain as your energy is kept in rather than being released. By exhaling naturally allows for more power kicking the ball and you feel your muscles working in the follow through, enabling you to put distance on the ball.

Feeling more comfortable? You are ready to experience something new about Relaxation …

Relaxation

"Our bodies are our gardens, our wills are gardeners."
William Shakespeare

Some people think of relaxation as sitting in front of the TV, going to the pub, spending time with family or friends. These may be relaxing times, but they still require a degree of emotional, mental and physical stimulation. True relaxation is a moment of emotional, mental and physical quiet. Breathing and heart rate slows, muscles relax and you feel calm and at peace in your body.

Here I will describe progressive relaxation, which is basically a relaxation routine where you start from the top of your head and work all the way down through the various muscle groups. Progressive relaxation was developed by Dr Edmund Jacobson sometime in the 1920's and is similar to the standard hypnotic induction as a way a person can easily relax their whole body from the top of their head, to the tip of their toes. It was an effective, but slow process which was modified by other therapists, mainly Richard Suinn, then Herbert Benson, both in the 1970's as a proven, simple way of relaxing the muscles of the body and mind.

Relaxation itself is valuable to health as it relieves mental and physical tension. When the body and mind are at ease, other mental skills become unlocked, then any progress toward mental training, self-

esteem, goal-setting and concentration can be smoothly accomplished by you.
Close your eyes if you want.
Take a deep breath and clench a fist tightly and hold for three seconds, imagining the tension in the fist as a colour, light or electricity, something which will represent the tension for you.
Relax your fist as you exhale slowly.
Imagine the muscle tension change colour, or change the substance, feel it dissolving or melting away. Notice the difference in you're hand before and after it was clenched and the relaxation you should feel now.
Do the same with the other hand and in the future, you can clench both fists at the same time.
Breath in slowly, carry on with the muscles of both arms, really tense them, imagine the colours or shapes, however you imagine the tension to be, then release and exhale as the colour or shape changes, let the arms relax and enjoy the feeling.
What other part of your body shall we relax next?
How about onto your face. Really scrunch your face up and notice how good it feels when you relax it.
Shrug your shoulders up, hold, then go through the relaxation procedure. Just let go.
Next your chest and back, start to feel like a rag doll.
Now onto your waist.
Proceed to your hips and buttocks, tense and relax them.
As you breath out, you might think about the feelings in your legs. Tense the thighs, let them go. Feel yourself sinking into the floor.
The calf muscles getting loose and limp, sinking down.
Finally you're feet, all tension draining away.
Isn't it interesting how your body relaxes without trying too hard. Enjoy the feeling of calm. You can go through this exercise as many times as you wish, just notice how relaxed you feel at the end.

***

You can also do relaxation quickly. Tense and relax the upper body as a whole, then the lower body , then the legs. Do this physical relaxation for a few seconds to stay alert and remain fresh mentally when the ball goes out of play.

You might even utilise this relaxed state by making positive suggestions to yourself.

Another way to do this is without tensing any muscles just before sleep as you lie in bed, as physically tensing any muscles may keep you awake. Imagine a wave of relaxation soothing its way down through you're body, maybe you can imagine a soft colour, one that can really relax you, going into every fibre of your body. Remember a time and place of peace, a sanctuary perhaps, gazing at the stars on a clear summer evening or lying on the beach, hearing the waves gently lap on the shore. Engage in the moment.

***

How about active relaxation. I'll illustrate this with a story. Several members of an athletic team were told to sprint 800 metres as fast as they could. The time was recorded. Next, the coach instructed them to sprint the same distance, only this time at just 90% of effort. Their time was better the second time. Why? Muscles are organised into opposing pairs. Running, as well as many other activities, is performed most effectively when some muscles are contracting, while others are relaxing. While sprinting at top speed, you use all of your leg muscles so they are actually working against themselves, accelerating and breaking at the same time. This prevents you running as fast as you can. As a paradox, running at 90% effort, you are contracting and relaxing the muscle pairs enough to stop them hindering maximum effort.

***

Here are some more relaxation techniques you can have a go at. This one is an ideal way to produce instant, physical relaxation which comes from Yoga. Breath through your eyes. That's right. Imagine as you inhale, the air you are breathing is entering your body through your eyes. You can actually feel your muscles relax even if your eyes are open, or shut. It happens all by itself!

Do you have a pet? Playing with an animal has proven to increase serotonin levels with a feeling of calm.

Close your eyes and remember a happy moment. If you can imagine a place in your body where that memory is stored, where would it be? Now find the cell in the middle of that area that holds that happy memory, imagine it smiling as it spreads itself outward toward the other cells of your body.

Meditate or do self-hypnosis for twenty minutes every day, it's the equivalent to four hours sleep.

Now you know how to relax, lets see how you Rest ...

Rest

"The ancestor of every action is a thought."
RALPH Waldo Emerson

WHEN we do sports, especially competitive sports, there is often damage caused to the body because the will to fight and the will to win makes the body tense and then injuries are caused along with illness.

Both your mind and body have their own way to rest and recharge their batteries. This happens about every 90 minutes when they stop external focus and spend around 15 minutes to rest and replenish. This is known as the ultradian rhythm. When you find yourself daydreaming and a soft feeling of comfort begins in your body is like that. Busy people constantly ignore these signs, so put themselves into overload. If you go with it, you will feel refreshed and have better concentration after.

Deepen the experience by self-hypnosis, meditation, or listen to relaxing music. Imagine yourself in a favourite place, an exotic beach, an oasis of peace and calm, a garden, somewhere that is special for you. Your nervous system cannot tell the difference between a real or an imagined event, so fool it into believing its on holiday.

Do this exercise to improve well-being once or twice a day, it does not take long and is a variation on the relaxation exercise I described earlier:

Put your attention on your feet and notice any feeling in them, coldness, warmth, weight.

Take a deep breath and as you exhale, imagine a warm, pleasant feeling begin in you're feet. You can imagine there's a colour.

When you are ready, take another deep breath and imagine that warm, relaxed feeling travelling up to you're knees. As it does, say a word like 'relax,' 'rest,' 'peace', or give each stage a number. Let that comfortable feeling penetrate you're muscles and bones, soothing them.

When you are ready, take another gentle breath and imagine the feeling rising up to you're waist and repeat you're special word or the next number.

With the same breathing pattern, let that feeling of ease and relaxation arrive at the shoulders, soothing them as you say that special word.

Next let that relaxation flow from you're shoulders down you're arms and into you're hands and fingers.

Again breath and let the feeling flow all the way up you're face to the top of you're head.

Say the word or number and let the feelings spread all over you're body.

In your mind say that word and imagine the relaxation double and float down from you're head so it mixes with those good feelings already going on inside you're body.

As this relaxation drifts down you're body, imagine any tension being washed down and away out of you're feet so it makes room for new, refreshing energy spreading down from you're head, until you feel you're body glow with energy from you're head to you're feet.

Now take a few moments to really bask in that feeling of relaxation.

If you want, do it again. The more you practice the better it becomes.

Just allow whatever happens to happen and feel satisfied with what you are accomplishing.

Maybe you will think about Soft Eyes ...

SOFT EYES

"The keeper was unsighted – he still didn't see it."
RON Atkinson

You will soon see the benefit of this technique as it gives you additional awareness of what is going on when there is a lot of movement happening around you. This technique has been used by experienced martial arts masters for many years as it helps them to remain calm and centred no matter what the situation they are facing.

If you have watched any old Bruce Lee movies, you may notice in the big fight scenes he often appears to be looking at his opponents feet. Actually he was putting his attention into a neutral area so he has awareness of any movement within his peripheral vision.

You use focused vision when you are concentrating your gaze on a particular object so you can see all the detail. Reading this book you are doing so with focused vision. This next bit is interesting. When you use focused vision it stimulates you're 'sympathetic nervous system' so your heart rate and blood pressure rise and you're blood vessels constrict. These are all part of the stress response.

On the other hand, using peripheral vision allows you to see the bigger picture and notice what is going on around you. Peripheral vision stimulates the 'parasympathetic nervous system' or the part that slows your heart rate, relaxes your muscles and increases gland and intestinal action, so doing away with stressful emotions.

You may appreciate, using your peripheral vision during a match will not only keep you calm while remaining alert, but importantly, peripheral vision helps you detect any movement happening 180 degrees or thereabouts around you. If you are a defender running back toward the goal while the opposition are mounting an attack, you need all round awareness to keep the back line solid.

For players in all positions, you can become aware of your team mates or any opponents around you, the right pass, where the opposition goal is from your position, if you are attempting a snap shot. Its simple. Here's how to do it:

> *The first time you practice, be in a room and over on one wall, place an object, a piece of paper perhaps, about 25 – 50 mm in diameter roughly at head height. Go over to the opposite wall and standing with your back to it, look at the wall ahead and gaze at the object and notice how far you can see around it.*
>
> *Here's the key to all this. Place your attention on the top, back part of your head, the place where someone would wear a skull cap. To help yourself, you can touch that top, back part of you're head first to give you a sensation of where to place your attention.*
>
> *As you fix your eyes on the object this time, while placing your attention on the top back part of your head, notice your field of vision has opened up. Are you aware of the wall either side of the object, above and below it? You should see most, or all of the wall facing, to the corners, the ceiling and the floor.*
>
> *Even though you are looking in the direction of the object, your awareness should have opened up to everything around it. That's soft eyes!*
>
> *Standing there relaxed, while thinking about that fixed point of attention at the back of your head, raise your arms out directly to your sides level with your head. Without moving your eyes from the object, are you aware of your arms? Wiggle your fingers.*
>
> *Notice how relaxed you may feel and your breathing is softer.*

Do the exercise a couple more times so you get familiar with it and begin to recognise the feeling of attention on the top, back part of you're head. At first, some people may feel a bit 'spacy' but they get used to it.

In training, practice using soft eyes as often as you are able until you begin to use it naturally. Once you get used to using soft eyes, you can lower your eyes as you would do with the ball at you're feet and remain alert to what is going on around you. This is something that does need frequent practice. Give it time and build up until you feel comfortable with the technique then you should be able to get into soft eyes instantly in a real match and it will also help you remain composed and in control of you're emotions.

Another benefit to the technique is in driving you're car. You will give yourself a much wider view of the road and become more aware of traffic coming up beside you.

Better answers come with Creative Questions ...

CREATIVE QUESTIONS

"If your not sure what to do with the ball, just pop it in the net and we'll discuss your options afterward."
BOB Paisley

ASKING questions is about the easiest and one of the most powerful tools you can use to transform yourself for the better and challenge you're mind.

Questions direct you're focus of attention. If your crossing is poor, notice how you question your crossing ability. Simply ask yourself "how can I ask this in a positive way?" which makes the questions more empowering.

Many sportspeople get frustrated because they ask themselves negative questions. "Why can't I … ?" To understand the question, the mind automatically looks for the reason why they cannot. But no matter what the answer is, they are still accepting the fact that they cannot do it. They are also reinforcing the problem in their mind. Here's a trick. Change 'why' into 'how.' Ask yourself "how can I do this?" This assumes it can be done and there can be a number of ways it can be done, so the question allows you're mind to search out a positive solution.

You will be delighted to discover how you can go further. You might ask "how shall I train with the cones today?" Instead ask "how

should I train with the cones today to improve ball skills and enjoy every minute."
So ask questions that focus on the positive:

How can my stamina problem be solved easily?
How can I stop inconsistent shooting?
How can I practice against being offside?
How can sport psychology make me a better player?
How am I going to become ... ?
These questions put your brain into a more resourceful state. If your not happy with an answer, change the way you ask the question.

Here is another one for you. When you want to know the answer to something, ask yourself the question about ten times and notice what you come up with. You're brain will keep searching until a happy solution is found. Its good to know that you're subconscious has the answer to all the questions you will ever ask. You can allow new answers to come to you.
Ask yourself these:

Do you love soccer so much you would pay to play it?
How passionate do you feel about soccer?
What would you do if you had unlimited ability?
Can you identify your ideal soccer role?
What difference would it make if you could improve 10 – 20%.

Curiosity creates questions. By bringing you're vivid imagination into play as you ask creative questions, you build up a vivid representation of the answer, then amplify it. Make it a sensory rich experience. Turn the colours brighter, the sounds louder, the feelings stronger. By regularly concentrating on what you want, you condition you're mind to attract more of it.

If you ever find it hard to bring an answer to mind, remember the solution to it! Remembrance was a Buddhist philosopher's trick. Instead of asking you're mind to search for an answer to a challenge, simply ask you're mind to remember it. Again the presupposition that you once knew the answer creates a mindset that the answer actually exists, so eliminates the anxiety of helplessness you may endure.

Many apprehensions and worries are caused by not giving you're mind something better to do. Look at it this way, the one asking the question is usually the one holding the cards.

Good answers from good questions often come to you about Goals ...

GOALS

*"People are not lazy.They simply have impotent goals –
that is, goals that do not inspire them."*
ANTHONY Robbins

CAN'T get enough now, can you? A goal is a mental representation of something you wish to achieve within a given time frame. Aiming for goals is a simple way to keep yourself motivated, evaluate progress, create emotion and achieve things. A goal can give you clearer direction. If you don't know where you're going, you will probably end up somewhere else. Talent will take you so far, setting goals goes with mental training and hard work.

Even with the greatest energy and enthusiasm, if you do not set specific goals, you're season could be directionless and unfulfilling. It is advisable that you set specific goals at the start of the season to avoid poor motivation and any downturns in you're mindset.

What would you do if you knew you could not fail? Goals can stop you stumbling through life. Why leave things to chance. Goals can help you move away from any limitations. Goals can make you the teams midfield general.

Focus your mind on a target and you are more likely to achieve it. If you do not aim for goals, your efforts (arrows) will go astray. Set time limits, but keep them flexible, reaching the goal is the important element, not the time frame. If you cannot reach the time frame, simply reassess the goal and keep on until it is reached. And focus on what you want rather than what you do not want.

To give yourself the best chance, you must understand how to set goals to improve any chance of success. Consider the following factors when forming goals, they help apply purpose to creating a 'well formed outcome.' Ensure they are stated positively and they are toward what you want, not what you do not want and that they can be well maintained.

A well known acronym for setting goals is SMART. The S is for specific. The more specific the easier it will become to figure if you are on target. Be careful about specific. "I want to score 20 goals a season" is specific. What happens when you have scored the 20? "I want to score more than 20 goals a season" gives you room to go further.

M is measurable. Create a start point from where you can measure your improvements.

A stands for achievable. Only you or your coach know if the goal is achievable. Is it too challenging or not challenging enough? Is it high enough to inspire solid hope of reaching it?

R is realistic. Do you have the resources and skills in you to bring you to your goal? Would more training be required? Do you have the confidence? If the target is too far away, it can damage your motivation.

And T is time-bound, an accomplishment date. By the end of the season is not precise enough. What day, month or even year do you plan to reach you're goal? Make it challenging.

Bring in all the senses of sight, hearing, feeling, even taste and smell when you form your goal. State you're goal in the present, as if it was already happening, exactly how you want it to be. Are there any negative consequences of you achieving you're goal? Think about it?

What do you want to accomplish in soccer? It starts when you set goals. It's the first step into putting you're dreams into action.

Ask goal oriented questions:
What do you want from soccer? Is it specific, definite, measurable?
Can you maintain the goal?
What stops you having that goal?
What resources have you? Are they emotional, financial, mental,

*physical, spiritual?
What resources are required?*

On a scale of 0 – 10, what would 10 be like as the very best? What would 0 be like? What is the closest to 10 you have been? Where are you on that scale now? What would it take to go 2 points higher? I bet you can do twice as good as you are doing.

How you design your goal makes a big difference. The bigger the better. Your goal should excite and scare you at the same time. If it frightens you a little, it shows you are facing your fear of failure, but you are not backing down.

Break the ultimate goal down into smaller parts until each step is easy for you to take action. By having a number of smaller chunks to work on stops you freaking out over a large overwhelming one. State goals with joy and act as if they were already a reality. Read or recite goals every day. Your mind needs constant repetitions to accept you're aims deeply and subconsciously. Be consistent.

When you set your sights on a goal whole-heartedly, your subconscious will do what it can to help you reach it. It does not take much to get things started, a simple thought or action. Or even better, a thought and action combined.

It is vital you believe you will achieve the goals you have set. The happier you are about them, you speed up the results. Do you want to achieve your goal so much you can almost taste it? Keep your dream alive with laughter and fun, if it becomes an effort, momentum slows. To support yourself and maintain motivation, celebrate or give yourself a small gift when you reach 80% of your goal.

Here is one goal you should aim for. Learn and practice the Rules of the Game, especially Offside. It is important playing in any position to understand totally the rules as they will have an influence on you're performance.

Goals give you growth. They can transform your life. Grab any evidence that shows you are achieving your target or that motivates you. Hold it in your hands, smell it, let it shine on you. Expect the cheers.

I cover more on goals in the Self-Hypnosis for Soccer section which comes later.

Lets change anything negative by reframing ...

Reframing

> *"Failure is an attitude, not an outcome."*
> Harvey Mackay

Failure is not the end result. Some people see failure as an excuse to give up, others think about failure so much, it becomes the best way to repeat it. Others, you included, can see things in a positive light by reframing any situation. The glass becomes half full, never half empty. You are in control. Reframing gives you the flexibility to make situations work for you.

In a trial, do you think you may never reach the required level? Do you worry you will lose your next game? Thoughts like these hamper performance. If you are afraid of losing, your dominant thought is about losing. Winners think about the next game and how to win it, losers think about the last one and who to blame. Notice your thoughts and change them into positives.

When you come across an opponent who is bigger, faster, or more experienced than you, don't tell yourself s/he is better than you. Use your internal dialogue to put the person down, ridicule them. Play on any weakness, real or perceived. Change their appearance, do you remember how to do that in the Imagination chapter? This gives your mind something better to do and gives you the confidence to face them. More relaxed, you can focus more easily on your strategy and stop any poor self-talk of fear or tension.

Positive thinking helps you realise there are limitations in any opponents ability as explained in the Imagination chapter. If your opponent is larger than you, tell yourself "being bigger s/he will be too slow and clumsy, there's no way s/he is going to keep up with me, I'm more agile, slimmer, faster."

If your opponent is smaller, maybe faster than you, its probable s/he will be physically weaker. "I'm stronger, I can easily win the ball." Look for their weakness, not strengths and create emotion when you speak to yourself. Be thrilled, believe you have the skill to defeat your opponent.

If you play with performance damaging thoughts, you are able to change or remove them. To make any negative emotion disappear, amend the thought. Change any colour, put a frame around it, make it smaller, further away, make it darker. Move the sound, change it. When you have changed the negative emotion, repeat several times so it cannot affect you again.

Another reframe can be done if you do not usually get pictures or sounds, but experience negative feelings. This is similar to moving the voice in The Inner Critic chapter:

Where is the feeling? Move it to your thumb, or big toe.
Does it have a shape? Change the shape.
What texture does it have? Change that.
What temperature has it? Make it cold or warm.
Change any element until all the negative feeling is eliminated.

Whenever you realise you have made a negative statement, restate what you just said into a positive by beginning the sentence with "in the past." So, "I always deliver poor crosses," can now become "in the past I used to deliver poor crosses."

Reframing can transform you, bring hope from hopelessness, turn despair into delight, build success from apathy. As with everything taught here, you have to practice, then practice some more, but once you have it, you have it for life.

New thinking = Better thinking = Better ability = Better you.

We often brand ourselves failure when we forget our successes. Look at any setback as an opportunity for a comeback. Change your thinking, change your soccer. Go for change, don't be afraid.

Reframing can help Internal Conflict …

INTERNAL CONFLICT

"Little things affect little minds."
BENJAMIN Disraeli

IMAGINE it's a penalty. You are the goalkeeper. To keep the net safe, do you go right, left or hope the shot comes straight at you? What if you're taking the kick? Part of you may have the confidence to accurately place the ball into the bottom left corner, while another part of you may want to be cautious, preferring to blast the ball with power. A tug-of-war is going on between ambition versus anxiety. If you are indecisive in your mind, how is your body going to know what to do?

If two incompatible states occur at the same time, you can modify each and reform them into a third state, which becomes an integration of the original two.

Throughout this book, you will learn methods which will get your mind working. Some may seem silly, others uncomfortable, some may challenge your way of thinking. Change does that. Take it as a good sign – its not for the faint-hearted.

This process can cause changes:

> *I'll use the example of the two conflicting beliefs above, confidence and caution, but you can use this on any other. Find a quiet place where you are not going to be disturbed and get yourself relaxed. Think about the situation causing internal conflict.*

Place your hands in front of yourself, palms up. Imagine the confident part in your dominant hand. Picture it as a colour, shape, a person, anything to make it real for you.
Do the same now with your other hand, where you place your cautious part.
Ask the confident part what its positive intention is for you. Continue asking until you get the feeling of an answer, even if you think your imagining it.
Next, ask the cautious part what its positive intention is for you.
Keep asking until you recognise on some level, that they both want the same outcome. Go through the process even if you think your imagination is playing tricks, its not.

This is for reference:

Confident part = more courage = responsibility = scoring = success.
Cautious part = anxious = safety = scoring = success.
Now imagine there is a Success Part there between your hands, possessing the resources
of confidence and caution.
Slowly bring your hands together until those two separate parts become an integrated whole.
Bring your hands up to your chest and imagine you are allowing the new integrated part to step inside you.
Convinced?

***

Next is a slightly different and quicker method to change a negative response into a positive:
Bring to mind a problem or bad memory you have. What would its solution or opposite be where you want a desirable outcome?
Place your non-dominant hand about 18 inches in front of your face and project your problem onto it. Have your dominant hand behind your back.
Practice by changing hands so your dominant hand is before your

face, while the other goes behind your back. Now project the solution onto your dominant hand.

Now you know the movement, get set up as before with the 'problem' hand before your face and as fast as you can, change hands. You can even use a motivational word or sound as you change.

Break state by shaking off your hands, repeating your phone number, or use some other distraction.

Repeat ten times. You should neutralise the problem and replace it with a beneficial condition.

As you practice this, it gets easier to resolve any internal conflict.

You can hold onto your seat as your entering the world where there are no limitations. Lets talk about motivation …

MOTIVATION

"What a great day for football, all we need is some green grass and a ball."
BILL Shankly

MOTIVATION is a much used word in sport. It comes from the Latin word meaning 'to move.' The most important thing for you however, is to love your soccer.

Most people can access unhappiness, guilt, even depression quite easily. By thinking of some failure in your life you open up undesirable emotions. The opposite can be the same. You can feel confident, excited, happy, you do not have to have a reason.

When you have played well in the past, you can repeat it by accessing the same levels of arousal that you experienced at that good time.

Here are some methods to increase motivation:

> Change livens things up, so you can vary your training routine, go for different exercises, a new location perhaps?
> Decreasing your rate of breathing will affect your nervous system. Slow, deep breathing through your nose creates relaxation in body and mind. Reread the Breathing chapter.
> Someone could call their nervous energy before a game anxiety. You could label it excitement. Rename nervousness, boredom,

drudgery, to something more inspiring. How does 'another type of excitement' sound, or 'adventurous.'

Release any tense, nervous energy by moving the muscles before a game. Tense and then relax each muscle group. You should do this during a warm up anyway.

Use key words that can excite or inspire you. 'Easy,' 'power,' 'winner,' even your name, team name or nickname. Create words or phrases that are personal, but powerful for you.

Use up-beat music to arouse you. On the pitch, play it in your head.

Suppose you have a boring task ahead of you. Picture something that motivates you, then trick your mind into changing the chore so it looks and feels exactly the same as the one that gets you going. As you've learnt, altering the variables, brightness, colour, position, shape, size, sound, can change how you react.

These are the steps:

Remember something that pleased you, a triumph you would wish to experience again. Maybe the result of your last cup game. Concentrate on that while you ask yourself:
Is it a still picture or a movie?
Is it in colour or black and white?
Is it close to you or further away?
What size?
Are you inside it, like the scene is wrapped around you, or outside and your looking in?
If any movement, is it fast or slow?
If the image is in front of you, are you looking from above, or below it?
Look at the boring task you want to feel motivated about. Ask yourself the same questions and notice what's different or the same about the two pictures?
Move the unmotivated picture into the space occupied by the triumphant picture. Change everything to make it look and feel the same as the triumphant picture.
Intensify it, make it vibrant. Give it more of what you have given it. Hear the band playing a theme tune. Even imagine pressure

on your back as if someone was pushing you into the picture. Make it real.
Do this change quickly, forcefully. Do it five times, breaking state between each change, so your starting as new, each time.

By telling your brain to represent the tedious picture in this exciting new way, the happy changes you make tell your brain "I don't want this ... I want this!" So, how do you feel about the boring task? It should feel better, more achievable.

***

Remember earlier, by changing 'why' into 'how' can be inspiring? Here's another word to change to get that motivation flowing. 'Should' gives people a feeling of guilt when they 'should do ... ' but don't. Turn it into 'want.' "I should practice corners," "I should concentrate facing a free kick." How do they make you feel in your body? Let it become "I want to practice corners," "I want to concentrate facing free kicks." Is that 'want' feeling now different from the 'should?' Has it made you more determined? Does it give you a prideful desire to achieve? 'Want power' can be as good as 'will power.'

As I have mentioned before, use language carefully. Words represent something, they are like symbols. Your words literary become your world. Here are some more you can play with. Turn 'but' into 'and.' "Great dribble but get your cross over quicker." That 'but' cancels out any good comment that came before it by sounding critical. Using 'and' keeps the comment positive.

'Try' and 'hope' are two words you must also remove from your vocabulary for the confusion they create in your subconscious. What you try and hope to do will be difficult and sets you up for failure. Here's why. If I ask you to try to pick up a ball lying at your feet and you do, you have failed. Why? Because I did not ask you to pick up the ball, I asked you to try. Have you ever felt uncertainty when someone asks you to try something? Now you know where that uncertain feeling comes from.

Read these two sentences:

"I will try to improve my corner kicks."
"I will improve my corner kicks."

Of those two sentences, the second resonates with the intention to improve and sounds more convincing. Put it like this, plants don't try to grow, they grow. Birds don't try to fly, they fly. Do you try to pay your club fee's or do you pay them?

When you hope for something, your subconscious automatically puts it into the unreachable section of your mind.

Turn 'if' into 'when,' 'why' can become 'because.' Here's some more: 'hopefully' or 'might' can become "I'm going to" and "I am capable." These words and phrases can be more motivating.

Complete these positive statements:

I am in the process of ...
I've decided ...
It excites me when ...

Lets investigate the power of Mirroring ...

Mirroring

"A champion is afraid of losing, everyone else is afraid of winning."
BILLIE Jean King

ANYTHING practiced continuously over time eventually becomes an automatic behaviour. Problems arise when the practice is not perfect. If its not spot-on, a player creates a varied pathway to the required standard, resulting in poor performance.

If your new to soccer, or about to play in an unfamiliar position, you have nothing to personally use as a reference to achieving a particular level. Copy the same things in the same way as someone who has excelled at it.

Choose a skill you would like to master. Imagine what having that ability can do for you. If you can, remember in the past having done the skill to the level you want.

Do you have a hero? Do you admire a particular player for his free kicks? Dribbling skills? Choose a role model, someone you respect and admire, who easily exhibits that skill. Someone who has walked that road.

Become a film director and make a movie in your mind of your hero demonstrating that skill effortlessly. Press play and watch carefully as your hero does everything perfect from beginning to end. Watch out for any distinctions you need to note.

Observe how your role model carries her/himself. How do they move? Imagine how they talk to themselves positively.

This time play the movie again, including yourself beside or behind your role model, imitating their actions, breathing, voice, mimic everything exactly.

Now climb in and disguise yourself as your hero, synchronise fully. Modify everything until the animation is exactly as you wish. See through their eyes, hear through their ears, take on the feelings of how empowered s/he is.

Feel what its like to be your role model having that skill. Build up the feelings, sounds, sights. See all around you how others respond.

How different does your future look. How much more optimism do you have as a result of this perfect skill? Live this future, make it real for yourself.

Step out and away and imagine in front of you the other you who now exhibit's the skills, assurance, energy you have made your own. Make any modifications.

If your role model has written instructions in a book or manual, or had themselves filmed, get a copy to study. Do research. Find out what that person has done to achieve success. Understand how they think.

Continue to rehearse until you are certain you can perform their skill automatically. Even if you feel like your making it up, your teaching your brain a new behaviour, so pretend until it becomes natural.

It is a valid thought that mirroring can oversimplify the topic of achieving success as it does not consider natural talent or social upbringing. For example, depending on your physical structure, you may never have the potential to become an international centre back. If you examine the world's greatest centre backs, you will find patterns in their builds, diets, lifestyles, training and thinking. Duplicating these patterns yourself is not a guarantee you will duplicate their skill level, but it will guarantee you will become as good a centre back as you can become, given your genetic potential.

Pretend you are an exceptionable soccer player, act as if it were true and soon your mind will forget to pretend, you've mastered it.

Feeling good? Want to create happiness on demand? You can with the Inner Smile ...

THE INNER SMILE

"I can let the team do the talking for me."
BOB Paisley

WHEN you are happy your body creates a chemical, serotonin, or the 'happy chemical.' It releases tension, controls pain, gives your immune system a boost and promotes well-being throughout your body.

Remember times when you were happy and light-hearted? If you cannot think of a particular time, how about remembering a comedy show or a film, even jokes you have heard. Go over them while you turn up the volume, the brightness, the colour, make it all richer and remember how good you felt until you find yourself smiling with pure joy. Double that feeling. Do it again. How do you feel?

Imagine now how better your life can be if you were like this all the time.

Vividly imagine your eyes smiling, feel a glint in them dancing. Raise the corners of your mouth as if you have a special secret. You use more facial muscles when you smile than when you frown, so give them a good workout.

Get a sense of where that happy feeling is the strongest. Play with it some more. Increase it. Give it a happy colour and roll it up to the top of your head and down to the bottom of your feet. Imagine every cell glowing with delight.

You can do this anywhere. Its good to imagine all the benefits this is going to give you, can it not?

Put a smile anywhere in your body that feels uncomfortable or tense. When you think about relationships, training, games, smile with that same energy and notice your mood begin to lift.

Here's a bonus. These happy chemicals create more connections in the brain every time you have a pleasant experience. So not only can your body experience happiness, the more often it happens, the more intelligent you become. What was a technique has now become a positive attitude.

And so the more positive you can be with relationships ...

RELATIONSHIPS

"Football is an honest game. Its true to life. It's a game about sharing. Football is a team game. So is life."
BILL Shankly

THIS chapter is on the basis of people you know involved in soccer.

Your fitness and health should be good, what about your relationships? The power of relationships are the food of life so you must be aware of the various relationship benefits and problems which can directly occur in your club.

There may be some individuals who are more concerned with themselves than the team, that spoils the closeness of the squad. It could be they have an iron-will and are determined to be the best, or get the best for their family if the club does not match their ambition. Some seniors may get bitter and jealous towards a skilful, young, new signing. Perhaps some members show a lack of commitment toward the overall team mission.

Accept there can be hard, challenging times ahead in your club. Its best to separate those from your personal life. Any negative feelings can rub off on those around you. Is it good to put loved ones through your disappointments? Best just to share the good times.

Some club's team spirit has reached legendary status, being so great it could be worth ten points over a season. In some cases being a team player can overcome any poor technical skill in terms of what can be contributed to the overall team.

Are there people around who will support you? Often its not the opposition that can be a barrier, but family, friends, work colleagues or team mates who are the problem. "You'll never be good enough" or "don't set your sights too high." As well meaning as they think they are, people saying those comments make a player worse than better. Have you ever noticed how expert some people can be about things they don't really have a clue about? If you take notice of people who tell you what you cannot do, you will never accomplish anything. Your placed in a negative frame of mind, have a conflict of priorities and it all spills over into a poor sporting performance.

You get intolerant coaches who think they are being helpful by criticising you. Some players respond well to that, but not all. "You'll never make it in soccer" doesn't work for everyone. Often you go onto the pitch and make mistakes because a negative expectation has been set up in your mind.

Less experienced players should be coached and encouraged by the more senior team members, they can work directly with juniors and lead by example. The junior players then have an opportunity to learn directly from their heroes, while the senior players learn more from coaching and working with enthusiastic juniors. A coach sometimes cannot give enough feedback to all the individuals in a squad, here, the senior players can see, advise, correct and encourage juniors.

Whether you are a professional or an amateur, if you want to live the life of an athlete you must dedicate yourself to soccer for nine months of the year. Yes, you can have a drink or two to wind down, but do it at appropriate times. Almost everyday, the sports pages print embarrassing and sometimes tragic stories of car crashes, drunken behaviour, drug suspensions, gambling. Lives and careers have been ruined by the poor choices sports people have made.

You cannot go clubbing. You will always get caught as there is always someone waiting with a camera. There is a vast amount of coverage today devoted to soccer players private lives. Some reporters will write anything for the sake of a news exclusive. There is a saying in tabloid journalism 'don't let the facts get in the way of a good story.'

Have you had an argument with someone, maybe the team captain and hours later you are still re-living it, still seeing the captains face and hearing the words. If you change the pictures and sounds as described in the chapter on Imagination, you can change your feelings.

What about a conflict of ideas with a coach, official or team mate? Perhaps you should consider what they have said before dismissing it. The truth can hurt sometimes, but putting yourself in others shoes, makes you adaptable so can give you further insight.

Go to a time when you had a difference of opinion with someone. Visualise that person stood before you now, notice all the details.

Now step out of your body and let any emotions go. This will soon start to make sense.

Step into their body and notice the world from their perspective, seeing, hearing, feeling and thinking from their point of view.

Next, step away from their body and let their feelings go.

Think of someone you admire. A friend, hero, saint, even a character from a book or the past who is mature, intelligent and wise. Step into their body and see that person considering you and your foe from a neutral position.

Are there any insights you can find. What advice would this mentor give you?

Lastly, step back into your own body taking with you anything you have learned. Can you move toward a resolution? Do you see things different?

***

A key to reaching your potential is learn to listen to others. Take advantage of the experience of coaches and senior players. They have faced the challenges you face and know how to deal with them. Lean toward them when they speak. Place your tongue on the roof of your mouth, this quietens internal dialogue, so you can pay attention to the other person. Don't interrupt or finish other's sentences. People will appreciate your listening skills. If someone interrupts while your speaking, politely ask them to wait until you have finished then you will listen while they speak.

Most footballers don't get to play in the World Cup. Follow your goals and not the crowd. You may feel envious when your friends go to parties, often the parties are not that much anyway. You can make up for it later. Avoid people and distractions that can turn you away from your dreams. Sometimes you may have to let go of old friendships if a fire to succeed in soccer burns in you.

One of the best ways to improve is mix with successful, skilful people. Surround yourself with achievers who provide good teaching and will make you better. Find a few people, players, referees, sports journalists, sport teachers, anyone who understands the game. Invite them out for refreshment or a meal. Be cheeky, write to them for advice. Let them know you want to pick their brains on how you can become successful. They become aware of you and understand you are serious. Be humble. Listen. As long as you are respectful, most people will enjoy the opportunity to help you. Other people can also see situations without the emotional baggage you may carry.

Ask those involved in the game to tell you what they would tell another player how to beat you. What are your strong points and weak ones. How they see you are vulnerable.

Praise others also. Being critical, judgemental, or opinionated are three ways to see relationships disappear. Use integrity. Impart sound knowledge and experience to junior players, set an example by being the best possible role model yourself. Develop their team spirit as well as guiding them to be better players.

We all get grumpy and out of sorts occasionally, so when you show up for training all excited and pumped up and find one of your team mates in a far less happy frame of mind, find out what is wrong. "Is there anything I can do" may be all that's needed for them to confide their trials and upsets. Most people having a tough time are not looking for a fight. When they know you are willing to be supportive, you will be appreciated.

Share your passion and love of the game. Excitement and passion are contagious. Do not allow others to put you off, or pull you down. And remember, scientists proved bumblebees could not fly. But the scientists didn't tell the bumblebees! You have more potential than you, or others realise.

Next let's look at the interesting subject of time management …

TIME MANAGEMENT

"Put your hand on a hot stone for a minute, it seems like an hour. Sit with a pretty girl for an hour, it seems like a minute."
ALBERT Einstein

YOU cannot control time, it just moves on. If you are a goal down during injury time, the clock still ticks away. You cannot buy it, save it, trade it or make it. Each and every moment passed is a moment gone that will never pass again. Your time, therefore, is valuable to you. The good thing is time is free.

If you cannot control time, you need to know how to manage what you do with your time. Learn to manage yourself. Remember your goals. Have you thought about them today? Remain focused on your soccer goals as it will help you arrange your days. Make decisions to accomplish what is important for you. That's a good reason to write goals down and review them frequently.

Most of us find it difficult to live in the present. We remember our past experiences and worry about future ones. Time passes at different rates for each of us. Your subconscious mind does not compare time passing by the same way as your conscious mind, which does so by a clock, watch or other timepiece.

Time varies depending on the circumstances you find yourself in. When you're nervous, in pain, sad, time slows down. The clock seems to drag. A couple of minutes are like half-an-hour, or time even seems to stands still. Long boring periods waiting for an important evening game can cause you to lose concentration and sharpness.

In contrast, when you are excited and happy, maybe having a great game, time flashes by.

So here is the ultimate time question to determine your soccer path. Are you willing to invest your time in yourself in order to make a grand return later? What choice will you make? Will it be the pain of commitment or the pain of regret? It takes discipline if you desire championships, champagne and shed-loads of cash!

***

You can manipulate time if you imagine a situation and slow the process right down to practice and improve a skill. I'll show you how. Lets take bending a free kick.

Get yourself into a relaxed state. If your better closing your eyes, do so. Hold a real ball in your hands if you can. If you can't, pretend you have one. Feel its weight, its coolness. Notice the pattern. Notice any smell.

Put the ball down.

Carefully examine the correct movement for bending a free kick. Feel for yourself the whole process, go through each step so you can physically remember the movements of run up, bringing your leg back, then the position of your foot as it strikes the sweet spot, hearing the connection. Bring in every sense as you feel more and more relaxed.

See each element in slow motion, at a snails pace so your technique is correct. Go over them several times making sure the feel of each element is just right. When your happy, speed it all up to real time. Imagine yourself take the kick as you would for real. Feel mighty, make everything colourful, vivid. Notice the goalkeeper, surprised and despondent as the ball flies into the net at a hundred miles an hour, exactly where you wanted it.

You can do this anywhere. With every mental rehearsal detail will increase. The practice you can make in your mind in a few minutes would require hours of practice in real time. Your subconscious cannot tell the difference between what is real and what is imagined, which is why this technique is perfect if you are out injured. It can help keep you focused.

Enjoy the activity as you see yourself perform at your best. And give yourself positive suggestions.

***

Here's another easy activity to help you place soccer as your number one daily activity. Get yourself a calendar, diary or inexpensive day planner. If it pictures soccer, much the better. Start your day with it by writing down the time you plan to train, play competitively, read a motivational book or magazine or watch a match. Plan the rest of your day around that event, no matter what. Make this a daily commitment. You have made soccer your top priority and arrange everything else around it rather than trying to fit soccer in.

In the next chapter you're going to learn to conquer fear ...

FEAR (FALSE EVIDENCE APPEARING REAL)

"Its not a question of getting rid of butterflies, it's a question of getting them to fly in formation."
JOHN Donohue

THE reason for much underachievement in sport is fear. You may have set goals, then done little or nothing to go for them. You worry or get frustrated about your performance, confusion sets in and positive thinking just does not help.

We all have a primary fight or flight response built into us for survival. This response will be explained more fully in the Pain Control chapter. We either fight, or flee from whatever is threatening us. Freeze and faint are more extreme experiences. Today, most of our dangers are not a threat to life and limb, but a psychological threat to our self-esteem and ego.

What I am going to discuss here is not a sporting technique itself, however some players go through anxieties during their soccer career. You may be uneasy in lifts, afraid of cats, dogs, birds. You don't like flying and your team is off to a foreign location. Worry about your most intimidating opponent who you soon have to face makes your stomach tremble. As you can see, fear creates limitations for you and can turn phobic.

You were not born with a fear or phobia. Many phobias can be traced back to an unpleasant incident when you were younger. Your elder brother may have locked you in a cupboard when you were a young child. What if the dark cupboard was full of moths, or even spiders? Since then, whenever you see moths or spiders or you are in an enclosed space, you relive the event.

Fear may be rated as the major reason why most soccer players do not fulfil their potential and it comes in all shapes and guises:

* *Fear of success*
* *Fear of winning*
* *Fear of failure*
* *Fear of losing*
* *Fear of making a mistake*
* *Fear of injury*
* *Fear of the unknown*

Lets consider briefly those aspects of fear mentioned above. These issues do exist in people's minds and thankfully, there are methods to deal with them. Why would anybody be afraid of success or winning? Some people with a low opinion of their ability become uncomfortable with success. They are stepping away from their 'comfort zone.' If a professional is frightened to death of public speaking, subconsciously they could sabotage their success to avoid any TV interviews. It is something not directly related to playing successful soccer, but certainly a consequence of that success.

The fear of failure, losing or making a mistake prevents people from reaching their full potential and creates a feeling of vulnerability. That fear of failure prevents most players from succeeding more than any opponent. Fear actually creates the situations that stop players from winning. A paradox in sport is that fear of failure actually makes failure more likely. If your dominant thought is you are afraid of playing badly in a cup semi-final, guess what the outcome is likely to be? The thought of the consequences inhibits you. Fear makes you play safe. Fear makes you play small.

An injury can create a fear response as you may be scared of hurting yourself again, then suffering through the agony of more recovery time. You may hesitate about going into a tackle after you damaged your knee in a previous game.

Some players might 'freeze' in a new situation or new surroundings. Its not what they are familiar with. Reaching the later stages of a cup competition when the opposition becomes of higher standard, when the venues get bigger, or playing in a hostile, crowded stadium creates apprehension.

Look at it this way, a fear, even a phobia, is an overcompensating protection mechanism. You did not learn it, you over-learned it and the good news is, because it was learned, it can be unlearned.

Your subconscious raises its head when you feel overwhelmed in any way. Warning you to be cautious, anxious, fearful. Now some lucky people can use these feelings as excitement. But you may be nervous about the first touch, a long pass, facing a free kick.

Acknowledge your subconscious, thank it for the warning, its done its job, now let it go. You do not need its presence, now switch your focus to getting on with the job at hand and take care of what you need to concentrate on. Concentration is a good antidote for anxiety.

***

This following technique was created by Richard Bandler and is known in NLP as 'The Fast Phobia Cure' or 'The Movie Theatre Technique:'

Close your eyes and get yourself comfortable. Give this your full involvement. Imagine you are sat in a cinema, you can remember a real one if you want. The screen is blank. Your in charge of a remote control, imagine it there in your hand.

On a scale of 0 – 10, 0 being nothing and 10 being extremely severe, how high is the problem your having?

In a moment you're going to play a movie of yourself and the problem you have. As it's a past event, the movie has aged, so it's poor quality and the colour has faded, even turned sepia. You will play your movie on a rectangle in the centre of the screen, not all of the screen.

Compose a comical theme tune, something like The Muppets, Monty Python, Popeye or similar.

Before you press play, remember a time when you know you were confident, excited or successful. Feel all that good energy and let it spread all around your body, now intensify it. Turn up the volume.

Maintain that good feeling while you watch the movie. You may even use anchoring to create a resourceful state if the fear your facing should get out of hand.

Now pay attention. Behind you is the projection booth. To get further distance from your fear, imagine yourself leaving your body sat there in the chair and floating up, back toward the projection booth. From here through the projection room glass, you can observe yourself watching the movie, watching yourself.

You will play the film of your bad event from beginning to end where it will then freeze-frame. Go ahead and press play on the remote.

When the film reaches that last frame, press stop. Now watch yourself in the cinema seat rise up and go up there to the still picture and congratulate the younger you for being so brave for going through and surviving the nasty experience. It's as if you see yourself from the fan's perspective. Your safe. With that acknowledgement watch yourself return to your seat.

When your ready, run the whole film backwards at top speed, hearing that comical music play. Then play the movie forwards then backwards at fast speed several times. How do you feel? Is there a difference to the memory? On a scale of 0 – 10 how low is it now? Has the old response gone? If so, float back down to your seat and feeling fully whole again, rise and exit the cinema.

We all get anxious at times, but people plagued by fear get anxious about being anxious. Accept fear and recognise it as the body's way of telling you to become energised. You can face any difficulty and come out smiling.

Check your arousal level with the Thermometer ...

THERMOMETER

"You have no control over what the other guy does. You only have control over what you do."
A J Kitt

CLOSE *your eyes. Can you remember a game when your playing or training perfectly in the area known as 'the zone?' What feelings are going on inside your body? What are you thinking? What words would you use to describe this event. Really get back to those good feelings so you are re-living them and as you do so, imagine in front of you a large scale, something like a thermometer for example, which reads 0 – 200. Can you say what the colour is and what are the shape and colour of the numbers?*

While you remember that time when you were playing at your optimal level, the reading of this scale will be set at 100. As you get back into that time and begin to feel good, anchor that feeling somewhere on your body, a wrist for example. You remember how to set resource anchors? If not, go back to the Anchoring chapter.

This time, recall a time when your arousal or anger level was too high for optimal performance. Once you get in touch with those feelings and emotions, imagine the scale reads 130 or 140.

To reach the optimum level of 100, inhale and use the words you just used describing your feelings and thoughts and as you exhale, say "relax" and watch the scale in your minds eye come down 15 or 20 points, half-way to the 100 mark. With another deep breath or two, have the scale reach 100 while your anchor is grasped to help you feel those good feelings. This can be repeated several times to train you in reducing the excessive high arousal.

Now remember a time when you had low arousal, poor motivation maybe. When you remember a time, imagine the scale is at 70 or 80. Again inhale and imagine energy coming in, exhale and imagine the energy flooding around your body as you call to minds those words and notice the scale rises 10 points. Do it again and see it rise to the 100 mark. This will be helped by firing your anchor again. Repeat that several times more.

Rehearse the breathing, using the correct words and using the anchor that bring you to 100 on the scale, that helps you achieve regular, frequent visits to your ideal optimum zone and it becomes automatic.

Or learn Spinning ...

SPINNING

"Life's too short to be afraid."
ROBBIE Williams

THIS is a simple, quick-fix technique taught by Paul McKenna, who I acknowledge here for it. You may find this worthwhile. Its ideal when you find yourself in a shaky or stressful situation which needs to be addressed there and then. The concept being bad feelings start in one place within your body and move in a prescribed direction. And so when reversing the direction of your bad feeling, you can eliminate it:
    Go through this routine while thinking about your problem. Say poor ability to judge an early pass. On a scale of 0 – 10, 0 being nothing and 10 being extremely uncomfortable, where are you at the moment?
    Think about what's disturbing you and get an idea of where that feeling begins. Usually, but not always its in the stomach/solar plexus area and moves upward toward your throat.
    Imagine lifting that feeling out of your body and watching it spin before you like a wheel.
    Imagine what colour it is. Now change that colour to your favourite.
    Maybe imagine a pleasant noise or music.
    With a flip, turn the wheel upside down so that it spins in the opposite direction.

When you feel calmer about the situation, pull the wheel back into your body to where it started, still spinning in the opposite direction.

Let it speed up, faster and faster, until the anxiety or upset begins to fade away and finally disappear. On a scale of 0 – 10, where do you find the problem now? Problems can vanish entirely.

You can also replace an undesirable state with a desirable one using Swish ...

SWISH

"I can change! You can change! Everybody can certainly change!"
ROCKY IV

THIS strategy can bring freedom to self-doubt. The trick is to have your positive image on the catapult in its high tension position, ready to fire, so that your mind accepts the image as going one way – toward you:

First, in front of you place a picture of an image you would like of yourself. Assertive, powerful, something that can give you goose bumps of excitement, or remember a memory you would wish to change. Something that is realistic and attainable.

Have your image full of the skills or qualities you would like more of, a natural dribbler, a midfield master. Make the details vivid, see yourself oozing with confidence, then make it larger, the colours bright, add sparkle, play a theme tune that's up-beat, adding vitality. Add approving voices of coaches and team mates. Make everything rich and intense. I really want you to live in this so include anything that improves the image.

Imagine this picture of your image has thick rubber bands attached to each corner and are fixed to a firing mechanism somewhere behind you. The picture is slowly pulled away from you, stretching off into the distance on those rubber bands, so that it seems like a giant catapult is being aimed at you, ready to fire. Lock that exciting picture in place and be aware of the tension in those stretched rubber bands. Your hands are on the firing lever.

Bring up a second image or a memory placed in front of you of whatever it is that's giving you a lack of confidence, inertia, fear, under-performance, where you would benefit from a new self-image. Lets say taking your eye of the ball. Drain away any colour, turn down the focus, shrink it down, quieten any sound.

Before you fire the first, good image, think of a motivational word. Originally it used to be 'Swish' as that is how therapists had the two images interchanged, but any word appropriate to you or the situation can be more effective.

When you are ready, feel yourself fire the catapult so that the exciting image shoots up, right in front of you, its acceleration tearing through that poor second image or memory, so that you end with that first exciting picture before you, replacing the poor one. If its done fast enough, you may even jump. Don't forget to add the inspiring word.

Notice any changes to how you feel. Reset the positive image by stretching back the elastic band again under tension so you have before you the remnants of the broken second image, that which made you feel bad. With that poor picture in front of you, fire again so that the good one once again rips through the bad, blasting through it once more.

Do this five times. Each time that first positive image shoots toward you, it ends bigger and brighter and the poor second image is gradually reduced until the last time, when it is completely destroyed to nothingness.

Another technique to reduce or eliminate problems is through Tapping ...

TAPPING

"Human feelings are words expressed in human flesh."
ARISTOTLE

A Meridian Energy System known as TFT has often been demonstrated by Paul McKenna on TV. These systems are safe, fast and easy to do. When you experience an emotional upset, you experience an imbalance in your body and by correcting that imbalance, you can go on to heal any emotional or physical issue.

Created by Dr Roger Callahan a psychologist trained in acupuncture, applied kinesiology and NLP, he devised TFT (Thought Field Therapy) in the seventies from insights belonging to those three fields, becoming a psychological version of acupuncture. Using a simple, painless procedure, you tap on particular acupuncture points on your body, so as you tap in the prescribed sequence, you distract your mind to reduce the unpleasant experience. TFT tends to use a lot of specific points tapped in a certain sequence.

Gary Craig, a master practitioner of NLP took TFT and distilled it into a simpler version known as EFT (Emotional Freedom Technique) which is much more widely used and is accessible for everyone as it uses the same points. Other therapists have further modified and refined the process. TAT, BSFF, Emotrance and some have modified EFT further. All deal with imbalances in the energy system.

All these procedures access the meridian energy system, where any emotions become trapped. The tapping creates vibrations in that energy system which appears to release the original energy disturbance and restores even flow, somewhat like tapping on your central heating pipes to clear an air lock.

Unconvinced? Like many of the techniques in this book, they seems strange at first, so are controversial, but they are based on scientific fact and have produced quick and substantial results for millions around the world.

For convenience, I will explain the system often demonstrated by Paul McKenna on TV as you may be able to see that programme as there are slight difference with the other systems.

While tapping, you must continue thinking about your problem throughout the whole sequence. This process can reduce or eliminate any strong, defeatist feelings, beliefs, bad memories, or emotions as it can physical symptoms.

Close your eyes and think about your problem. Lets say you always head the ball poorly. You have painful accounts of heading like you have a cocked hat on your head or even ducking a high ball coming toward you. On a scale of 0 – 10, 0 being nothing and 10 being the worst it could ever be, where is your problem?

Keep on thinking about the heading problem, take two fingers of either hand and tap firmly 10x above one of your eyebrows.

Now tap under that eye 10x. Still thinking about the problem.

Now tap 10x under your colour bone.

As you continue to think about your problem, tap under your armpit 10x.

Tap on the 'karate chop' side of your other hand.

Tap on the back of your other hand between the knuckles of your ring finger and little finger.

Open your eyes, then close them. Keep tapping while you continue to think about the problem. The following eye movements are connected to various brain functions. Open your eyes. Look down to your right, then centre, then down to your left.

Keep tapping and as you do so, rotate your eyes 360 degrees anti-clockwise, then 360 degrees clockwise.

Still thinking about the heading concern, hum the first few lines of

Happy Birthday or a favourite tune. This humming allows switching between right brain hemisphere – left brain hemisphere – right brain hemisphere activity.

Next, count aloud from 1–5.

Repeat the first few lines of Happy Birthday or your favourite tune.

Still thinking on the problem, close your eyes and tap 10x above your eye again.

Again tap under your collar bone.

Tap under your armpit.

Finally tap on the 'karate chop' point again.

Where is your problem regarding heading on the scale of 0 – 10? You should have it down to a manageable level by the second go. If it has not reduced, go over the sequence again. It depends on how strong your problem was to start with, so it might need several attempts to reduce or completely eliminate it. Repeat as needed. You may get confused about what used to bother you.

Now I'll show you how the future can be your friend with Time Line …

Time Line

"If my mind can conceive it, and I can believe it, I then can achieve it."
Larry Holmes

PART of you that is curious may wonder about this experience. Think of a time ahead when you can see yourself celebrating a success, how about Player of the Season, or holding aloft a trophy as captain while you celebrate with your team mates, the champagne corks popping, your supporters cheering, see and hear the fireworks. When you imagine that kind of future, your subconscious is directed toward making it happen.

Devised by Tad James, another great psychology pioneer, a Time Line is explained as an imaginary line where events happen and even where your subconscious stores memories. This line stretches off in one direction to your future and in the opposite direction for your past. Examples of this would be when you say "I'm looking forward to the game" or "I'll put this defeat in the past."

There are two parts to this exercise. First, how do you represent time? Think about something you do every day, if its soccer related so much the better. As you see yourself doing this activity tomorrow, notice the direction you looked. Was your future in front, or was it to your left or right? Higher or lower. How far away?

Think about doing that task next week. Is the image further away, in front, behind, to the side? Higher or lower? Stay with me on *this. What about a week ago in the past? Where were you doing the activity then?*

Think about doing the same thing a month in the future. Is the image closer or further away? More in front or behind, more to one side or another? How about a month ago?

You can go on imagining the same activity three, six, twelve months in the future. Where is the picture?

Imagine all these pictures are dots joined together by a line, flags or cones as if you were connecting the dots inside your mind. This is how you subconsciously see time, your Time Line.

The second part of this exercise is creating your soccer future, then moving into it. Project yourself several months into your future, maybe the end of a rewarding season. See from your minds eye, out. Or maybe you have reached a goal. Everything has gone well, your game has improved, your more confident, your more knowledgeable. You also have achievements in your life outside soccer.

Be curious about your future. Form an image of that ideal scene of everything you wish to happen in your future. It can be real or symbolic. See yourself there, happy and successful. Make the image big, bright, bold, richly coloured and anticipate how good you will feel the sparkle.

Now fill in the steps along the way to this ideal scene. Make a smaller image and place it a few weeks, or months before this final big picture. Keep doing this until you have a succession of images connecting the present to your ideal future so that they get bigger each time, with good things happening along the way.

Look at those pictures you have created as stepping stones and imagine floating up out of your body and into each picture, spending a few moments living in each one to absorb the positive experiences happening there.

When you reach that final image, really get into the feeling of achievement as you discover yourself already there.

Finally return to the present and look along your future Time Line. Have confidence in the knowledge that it is a map for your subconscious to bring fulfilment to the future you have created.

Next, lets talk about Pain Control …

Pain Control

"Listen son, you haven't broken your leg. Its all in the mind."
BILL Shankly

No medical claims are expressed or implied here. You must only use these pain-control techniques when you know the cause of any pain. Whatever the results you get, please continue to take any medication or actions prescribed by your health practitioner. Pain means there is something wrong. If there is something wrong, you must find medical assistance.

If you suffer pain or discomfort in any part of your body, just fifteen minutes of this exercise can make it disappear or diminish it significantly. Using the power of their mind, people who performed the exercise which follows, were able to reduce pain by up to 80%. Want it to happen, expect it to happen, allow it to happen.

A closed eye process is best, so learn the method first, or have someone read it to you. The purpose of this exercise is to look at the pain from a different perspective so you look beyond the pain.

Get yourself relaxed, somewhere you won't be disturbed. Without being cynical, without judging if you are doing it right, dismiss your rational mind and locate specifically the condition your suffering.

Now describe it. How big is it? How long, thick, wide? What shape is it? A cube, flat, rectangle, round, square, triangle, is it jagged? Is it dull or sharp?

Just keep focusing on the condition. Describe exactly what it feels like. Pounding, pressing, pulsating, stretching, tearing?
Does it have a colour to you? A smell? A weight? If your not sure, just make it up.
Is there a temperature?
Now you have the location, shape and sensation of the condition? Does it move?
Answer this – are you willing to let this condition go?
If yes, I want you to go inside your body and take it out. You can read that sentence again. Just imagine your reaching inside your body and taking the 'thing' out.
With your eyes still closed, imagine it in your hand. See the colour, the shape. Is it hard or can you mould it? Roll it up into a ball, go on, play with your condition. Toss it up into the air a few times and when you are ready, kick it away saying "goodbye'"to it or "this no longer bothers me.'" To your surprise you can get rid of it.
Now look inside. Are the symptoms still there? The same or changed? Lets focus on it a while longer.
How big is it now? What colour? Shape? Reach in and take it out of your body. How does that feel.
Hold it in your hand. Can you bend it? Drop it on the floor. Does it make a sound? Does it smash into pieces? Pick it up and roll it into a ball again. Tell yourself you no longer want it and kick it away.
Is the condition still there? Know that you can do the process again. As you reduce the condition, mentally you get stronger and you can speed up recovery.
Gently get centred back into your body and when ready, open your eyes.
You can also use that exercise on emotional issues of anger, grief or fear.

***

I'd like to introduce you to Noesitherapy – healing by thinking – and here credit the founder Dr Angel Escudero, a surgeon in Valencia. He has been investigated by medical experts the world over who have praised his method. He has lectured to the medical world and has been featured on a number of TV broadcasts around the globe. Dr Jonathan

Royle who taught me, uses Noesitherapy as part of his Complete Mind Therapy.

The theory behind Noesitherapy stems from the fight or flight response. Back in time, the caveman developed the fight or flight response as a way adrenaline flowed throughout the body. The muscles were then strengthened so he could fight more vigorously or run away more quickly. So our caveman was constantly on full alert, especially out hunting. He would fight an opponent or an animal, but there would still be fear, so his mouth would go dry, muscles would tense and he would have extra strength due to the physiology of the body. When he defeated his foe or killed the animal, he would sigh with relief.

If he met an animal that wanted him for its dinner, then flight would be the action. If he managed to get away, he sighed with relief and notice again his mouth was dry. That's the key. After any stress is over, saliva returns to the dry mouth. We also sigh and the muscles relax, I'll not get involved here with the other physical signs of heart beat, sweating, blood pressure, digestion, which is thousands of years conditioning in us humans, who now live in a different age. Just remember the saliva.

It's the apprehension, fear or expectancy of feeling pain that makes pain hurt or exist at all. You finish a DIY task and go to the sink to wash your hands and see blood. You felt nothing when the cut happened as your mind was somewhere else. The moment you see blood, the cut starts stinging and funnily enough, bleeds more.

If you're injured and told you have to live with a certain amount of pain, then being able to reframe your mind so there's no pain, maybe just a little discomfort, makes it more bearable.

Use the 0 – 10 scale to judge how much pain your experiencing.

Besides breathing deeply, your body is conditioned to relax with saliva. Use the idea of a lemon to get saliva working in your mouth. Lets suppose your right ankle is injured. Imagine your eating a big, yellow, tangy, juicy lemon. Get the saliva on your tongue. This part is going to sound daft I know. Say to yourself, aloud if you can, while the saliva is on your tongue, "my right ankle is now completely anaesthetized" which you say three times. Why three times? The concept behind that is the first time you say it your subconscious may ignore the conscious command as its busy with other tasks. Ask a second time, your subconscious realises you are there and begins to process and the third time the subconscious knows its true and activates in a way that is right for you. Besides, Dr Escudero does it with his patients and he then carries out amputations!

Take a nice, deep, relaxing breath. Imagine your right ankle has gone cold, its like a lump of meat from the freezer. No discomfort to concern you. In a moment you can swallow the saliva, just say a few affirmations to yourself, such as you feel no discomfort, you can turn off pain like a switch. Where is the pain now on the 0 – 10 scale?

***

There are lots of studies that have been carried out using hypnosis for pain relief and even performing operations without anaesthesia. One of the easiest methods for using hypnosis in pain control is Glove Anaesthesia:

Find a comfortable place where you will not be disturbed. Get yourself relaxed and close your eyes. Focus on your breathing, allowing it to be slow, deep and steady. Imagine relaxing all the muscles in your body one by one, beginning at the top of your head, going all the way down to the tips of your toes. Be aware of each muscle in your body melting, softening as you feel more and more relaxed.

Imagine you are in a favourite place, somewhere peaceful and safe. Imagine you can see the sights, hear the sounds, feel the feelings you would feel there. Take your time.

Using self-talk, remind yourself you have the ability and power to be in control of any sensations in your body. Because you do! Accept you are in control of your mind as you focus on the unlimited power of your mind. Tell yourself you can send numbing sensations into any part of your body. Believe in yourself and the power of your mind as you encourage and empower yourself. Believe these words are being delivered into the deepest levels of your mind. Imagine they are being accepted on every level of your body and mind.

Concentrate on your dominant hand, really concentrate on it. Notice all the tiny sensations you feel there. Begin to imagine using your concentration your hand will become free of all feeling. Maybe imagine your hand is encased in ice, really imagine that.

Continue to place your attention on your dominant hand and allow it to lose all feeling. Tell yourself your hand is becoming number and number. No feeling at all. Be aware of all the unusual sensations there in your hand as it goes to sleep.

Tell yourself every breath you take causes your hand to become number and number until you cannot feel your hand at all. You just cannot feel your hand at all. No feeling. Numb.

When you are sure you have developed the correct level of numbness in your hand you can transfer that lack of feeling to any injured part of your body. Raise your hand and place it upon the part of your body you want to feel numb. Notice it becomes cool and numb. Maybe imagine that numbness as a colour and it is spreading all over that area. Feel like you are releasing all those sensations of numbness into the injured area. Give yourself a time limit this will last for. You do not want that part to be numb for a lifetime so make sure you set yourself a time limit when the anaesthesia will end.

When you have transferred the calm, soothing, healing numbness, really enjoy the sensations as the area gets better, relief flowing through the area. Now say the word 'anaesthesia' so that each time you say the word in future occasions your mind has the correct intention and resources to send recovery into the injured area. Believe each time you use this technique in the future, it will enhance your recovery, getting better each time.

You now know how to use pain control on your injuries and illness ...

Injuries & Illness

"Adversity causes some men to break; others to break records."
WILLIAM A Ward

ANYTHING you read here is not intended to replace medical advice you are receiving from a health practitioner. Any injury, no matter how minor, needs to be evaluated for prompt diagnosis and treatment. This can prevent a minor injury evolving into a major repetitive problem.

There are preventive measures you should be aware of to avoid stiff, sore muscles and aching joints. If you are with a professional club, you will be aware of these. Any aggressive training or repetitive overload will eventually over-stress ligaments and tendons so making joint instability more likely, along with the added risk of inflammation. Massage treatment can reverse some problems, however, also include plenty of vitamin C, vitamin E and beta carotene in your diet.

Three or four weeks into a serious injury, denial, then depression begins as there is generally a long time period before any progress seems to happen and before you begin to show recovery. Fear creeps in, especially fear of the unknown as you don't know how long you are going to be out. How safe is your position in the team? And what makes it worse is you are expected to act manly about it. But with all that uncertainty going on in your head, your anguish is doubled.

Following an injury, especially a serious one, many players often experience the fear of re-injury

All injuries need a chance to be rested and recover as living and playing on pain killers and anti-inflammatory tablets will eventually cause long-term damage. Players in Britain are so determined to get back to playing that they do so before making a full recovery. In most countries abroad the attitude of players is it's no point playing if you are not 100% fit.

Besides the correct medical treatment, you can help yourself by maintaining a positive mind set, rather than walking around aimlessly staring into space. If you are suffering a long-term injury, talk things over regarding how you feel with someone at your club.

You can become a slave to your mind and emotions. What you say to yourself can be a major key to recovery. You can literally talk yourself into health or sickness mentally, physically and emotionally. "I always get sick this time of year" can act like a self-fulfilling prophesy.

Avoid those dark moments haunting you as you question if you are ever going to recover. You can accelerate your bodies natural healing by visualising your body healing itself. Your subconscious mind runs your body from a blueprint of perfect health.

One of the most common injuries in soccer happens to the knees. Sudden deceleration, combined with a sudden change in direction applies forces to the to the anterior cruciate ligament. This happens much more often in females than males. The female pelvis is wider than a male, so the angle of the knee is slightly more knock-kneed, therefore creating more stress on her knees.

In the past, there was a lot of focus on strengthening the quadriceps to stabilise the knee joint, but modern times have seen a rethink in favour of a more balanced development of both the front muscles and back muscles of the leg.

To slow down and change direction simultaneously, you need to strengthen your posterior muscles, the hamstrings, gluteals and gastronomies. Backward walking can help, backward pedalling or walking lunges.

If you feel pain or undue stiffness, get it looked at. Lets suppose you generally take all the free kicks. You feel pain in your knee. Running is ok, it's the kicking that causes the discomfort. But it's still a case of wanting to play and not let the side down even if you have a little 'niggle.' There you are later with a repetitive injury. All that kicking dead balls has taken its toll.

Its tough if you find yourself out through injury. You can do nothing during recovery, or use your time wisely. Use any period of forced inactivity to study and further your knowledge. List the things you can do, perhaps studying DVD's, or reading. Perform any exercise you can do, even if its riding an exercise bike with your arm in a sling. Practice muscle relaxation routines and mental training which will improve your psychological performance and make you more prepared when you resume playing.

Remain involved with your club. If you are able, go along to the team games and cheer on your team mates, attend training sessions and contribute to team spirit. If possible, get yourself up to the top of the stands at games. You see things from a completely different perspective there that you would not normally see from playing or sat on the bench.

Run videos in your head of yourself doing well. It keeps your mind focused and positive. Your mind stores what you have experienced and what you have thought the same way. This is perfect for mental training. You can train using visualisation to sharpen good technical and tactical techniques. The advantage is you can go through several repetitions of any technique in minutes in your head without causing further injury.

No matter how confident you are, injuries do plant doubts in your mind, which is why the mental side of recovery is so important. Now its important for me to make this next distinction for you – **your not injured anymore! You're in a state of recuperation!**

How about an injured opponent? Is it real or exaggerated? Ignore anything they say. Assume its for gamesmanship, sympathy or heroics. Give them no attention until after the match. If your opponent can stand on the field of play, they are fit enough to warrant your best efforts. If their injury is real or not, it can still have a negative influence on you.

Stress manifests itself in all kinds of disguises including illness. Vomiting before an important game to being nervous about being dropped. An upset stomach from a fear of being transferred, to reading about your actions in the local paper. You do, of course, have a physical release by playing and training, but when you turn to management and coaching, that physical release is often no longer available.

Recover with Simulation Training …

SIMULATION TRAINING

"In football everything is complicated by the presence of the opposition."
JEAN Paul Sarte

BY creating game situations in training which are as real as possible, allows soccer players to practice their performance reactions to the various difficult match situations they would encounter, while maintaining their concentration, so being better prepared to face all competition demands. This way they are more able to confront physical, mental and technical challenges.

Simulation training helps soccer players better understand what they are capable of in real game situations and able to adapt to distractions and demands when they are introduced at the training session. Even if this is not possible in the real world, it can be practiced through vivid individual or group mental training.

The team should train outdoors in the weather conditions they would normally face. Rain, sun, heat, cold, wind, all have an affect on performance. They must be prepared as much as possible by dressing and training for the weather conditions they will encounter in their forthcoming games. Even if it means travelling early into the same time zone and climate if about to compete abroad.

Individual players should learn to react to coming from behind, coming on as a substitute or being substituted. A last minute change in tactics, or anything that can distract, so the player can remain calm and focused throughout. Expect more in simulation training than would happen in a real game. A practice game against the reserves could start with the first eleven three goals down so they become used to fighting back from coming behind. To take this further, there could be one or two more reserves on the pitch than the first eleven have, so they are used to playing against more men.

Longer, harder training matches are not advised before a game as more recovery time will be required by the players. Besides longer training matches, exercises can be developed where the players can only use their left foot, or only have two touches on the ball. Have one player compete against two during set-piece exercises.

Relax as you push through personal barriers. Your mind must be able to overcome physical discomfort. Push through personal discomfort in training, even include pain during any mental rehearsal so you can perform beyond it. When a player knows and expects to feel pain, they are more able to accept it. Success often depends on the players ability to tolerate the distress of heavy, hurting, burning muscles during extra time to win medals.

Pre-plan what to do when the opposition does A, B, or C. Use video of forthcoming opponents to analyse their moves and study individual star players. Some of your team can role play the future opponents during a training game, or rehearse set-piece situations to better anticipate how the opposition will function.

For real and mental rehearsal, the team can imagine they are playing in an important game. Go through the normal sequence of preparation, warm up, going through the whole event, all as if being at a key game. Include bad referee decisions, officials arguing, flash photography, PA announcements half way through a move, or any other distraction so the players become used to them.

Poor referee decisions during training matches will better prepare players to overcome frustrations and the temper tantrums we see on the field. If the players can learn to control themselves, they can remain focused to tactically deal with their opponents next move and concentrate on what they do have control over.

A player can use this to imagine they are a higher quality player, matching their role models qualities, execute their movements and skills, integrating posture, composure, even repeating words or phrases spoken by their hero.

The advantage of simulation training is the players are exposed to expected and unexpected situations they can face during a real competitive game. This training has the players do more than is normally required, so they can develop the confidence to remain focused under difficult circumstances. Well thought out simulation training will prepare players, providing they are not overloaded into overtraining which will only burn players out, increase injury risk and take away the joy of the game. Adequate rest and recovery must be respected to get the best from the players.

Stay motivated with a soccer scrap book ...

SOCCER SCRAP BOOK

"Peak performers from various fields maintain their childlike qualities!"
LARS Eric Unestahl

ANYONE wanting to invest time in soccer is advised to learn as much as they can about the
game. Read books, newspapers, magazines, watch DVD's. Take clippings or photo-copies of pictures, diagrams and photos. Collect brochures, programmes of anything to bring into your soccer life.

Every time you look at them, it reminds you of the goals yet to achieve, your role models, places you would like to play, equipment you would like to own. It keeps an account of your football activities, training logs, events, symbols, anything that gives you motivation and support.

Do the same with a video/DVD scrap book. Watch the top players, study what works for them.

Use soccer bookmarks. Drink from a soccer mug. Dream in soccer bedding.

Keep larger items around your home or room that act as powerful anchors. Look and handle them frequently. Use regular rehearsal time to smell and feel the texture of the ball. Give yourself a sensory-rich experience. Concentration and rehearsal brings in countless nerve impulses.

Going slightly further, it may be helpful to concentrate on an object, a ball, shirt, corner flag, even a poster on your wall. Study it while being relaxed. Use the exercise like a meditation session. When you notice your thoughts begin to wonder, return your full attention to your object. This exercise will improve your ability to focus and give you awareness of where your mind goes.

Get a picture of your hero in action, an exceptional goalkeeper, a defender of high quality, or a forward. Splice a photo of your head onto their body. Put it somewhere you can view it often. You may not posses all your hero's qualities, but your empowering your mind and stretching it beyond any limitations. Read the Mirroring chapter again, then copy and pretend until you become your own hero. Learn from the legends.

Do you have any superstitions ...

SUPERSTITIONS

"Luck is what happens when preparation meets opportunity."
DARREL Royal

THE world of soccer is made up of numerous influences and variables, equipment, tactics. The intricacies from Mother Nature and the ever-changing game dynamics that we cannot predict or control, would have some believe that luck and not talent is the main ingredient for success.

Some individuals will use lucky rituals and routines no matter how bizarre, to bring order and stability to their world and keep them from harm, or accident in a belief that skill and physical condition are not enough to defend them from danger.

With practical wisdom, superstition can be reassuring, as it makes sense to have some order. You may already have a routine for laying out your kit, inspecting your boots or examine your fixture list. Have you ever thought about your preparations and come across something you normally do, but didn't? The result can sometimes bring negativity and self-doubt before the game begins followed by fretting, wondering and worry.

You may have a ritual such as a particular eating habit or are you fussy about a favourite article of clothing you always wear? Perhaps you have a lucky talisman, a horseshoe or a four-leaf clover fixed onto your shin pads. A player often emotionally attaches success or failure to these un-rational rituals hoping they can enter the performance zone prior to a match.

Not all superstitious behaviour is healthy. It is often difficult for someone to recognise that routines which worked in the past have no longer become useful. Taking superstition to extreme can lead to rigidness and magical belief so that some players can get completely distressed if their routine is upset and lose confidence in themselves.

A player who dons and fastens each piece of clothing and equipment in exactly the same way every time, may have to undress and start again if something happens to take him out of sequence.

There is no such thing as luck, only the perception of it. The more dedication, preparation, research and training you do, consistently and persistently, to get you to your reward, the more chance you have of creating your own luck.

The more you practice the luckier you get. There is an aspect to every game that you cannot control, so for a great performance you need that something extra. That something extra comes from the long, hard, training you have spent to develop your skill, luck does not come into it.

You may know plenty of players who think once they get a bad run, it will continue, or when on a good run, they expect it to end. Once you get into a run of success, there is no logical reason why it cannot continue. You will go into a barren patch sometime, it does not last when your thinking is right. Class is permanent, bad form is temporary.

See yourself in daydreams ...

DAYDREAM

"Yes Arjan, I dream. For only those who can dream can make their dreams come true."
BHUVAN Laagan

As you enter the stadium from the players tunnel, a sea of colour greets your eye's as you hear the crowd's roar. You look to one side and below the glare from the stadium floodlights you feel the energy from your supporters as they sway and sing in jubilation. With pride you notice every cell of your body seems to be tingling with excitement. Smelling the freshly cut pitch your excitement grows as you hear the announcers voice echo as he begins to read out your team. You hear your name. You see your name on the waving, silken banners. Your name!

One of our luxurious pleasures is daydreaming. You see yourself as the James Bond of the soccer world. You dribble around defenders faster than a launched missile, your tackling is more ferocious than Odd Job. Injured and limping, your penalty kick wins your team the cup in the last few seconds of the game. You're the hero!

It does not stop as you get older. Your dreams may become more modest and limited. Now you join a failed team as a no-nonsense coach, introducing revolutionary techniques and tactics. You right all wrongs as you conquer the soccer world.

Would you call it wishful thinking? I would say it was subconscious rehearsal. Daydreaming, visualisation, imagination, call it what you will, when you engage in them, you should bring in all relevant sights, sounds, feelings, smells and if appropriate, tastes. Make them full of life's rich juices.

Your soccer daydreams can be great fun. Just like visualisation mind training, some almost impossible feats begin with daydreaming. You are still mentally rehearsing your performance. Therefore daydream everything going right travelling to the ground, during the game, before going to sleep while at home, staying in a hotel before a game, anywhere and anytime.

Using any form of mental imagery provides a positive emotional training aid which can help you achieve positive results, because they communicate to your nervous system very clearly your desires to see yourself excelling. By daydreaming, you have the opportunity to get things right, so reinforcing to your subconscious the habit of winning.

End of play is upon us ...

FULL TIME

"I was only in the game for the love of football."
BILL Shankly

TIME! Being physically fit and technically adept is only part of being prepared in soccer these days. Mental and emotional strength are also required. I have covered mind techniques that can change your soccer, not just now, but progressively for years to come. This was written with soccer in mind, however, many of the methods described are able to cross over into other areas of your life. As you become familiar with them, your energy and motivation will improve.

If you do nothing, what will happen? If you do something, what will happen?

We are all faced with opportunities disguised as impossible situations.

Even a small change to your thinking can make a big difference. As you continue with the new way, you will begin to realise how much you have changed. Don't look how far you have to go, rather how far you have come. As you have learnt, the conscious mind can only think of one thing at a time, why not make it something positive. You can, can you not?

You're often the last person to notice any change. Keep an ear open for comments from friends or soccer colleagues. Maybe they will comment on how happy you have become lately, how your passing is improving, or your becoming a confident, well rounded player.

You should make this book important enough to return to it several times to get the results you need. Why not carry it around in your kit bag. No single technique is a magic pill, but when you practice them repeatedly, they will become familiar. You can even go to the beginning and start reading again.

When I was learning to drive I practised again and again until I was confident enough to pass my test, just as drivers before me had done. All I needed was the confidence practice would bring. I did not assume driving would not work on my first attempt! Please keep that in mind. If a method does not work on your first attempt, don't give up on it. Understand these tried and tested techniques do work. They work beautifully. You may even find one an exciting and rewarding activity.

Imagine staring into a mirror after a match and honestly telling the person you see there, you did your best. Feeling the pride and joy of a perfect performance. The delight you have created for your team mates, the fans, the directors, your coach, your mind coach – sorry about that blatant 'sales plug.'

I sincerely hope you enjoy what has been presented here and I really want you to succeed, because by your success, this book will be judged. Have fun and enjoy your soccer.

Some suggestions were indirect, embedded into the text to place them into your subconscious mind.

The time to start using them is now ...

BIBLIOGRAPHY

Bolstad, Dr Richard., Resolve.
Callahan, Dr Roger., Tapping The Healer Within.
Court, Martyn., The Winning Mindset.
Eason, Adam., The Secrets of Self-Hypnosis.
Edgette, John H & Rowan, Tim., Winning The Mind Game.
Hodgson, David., The Buzz.
Lazarus, Jeremy., Ahead of the Game.
Liggett, Donald R., Sport Hypnosis.
Mack, Garry with David Casstevens., Mind Gym.
McKenna, Paul., Change Your Life In Seven Days.
Mycoe, Stephen., Unlimited Sports Success.
Orlick, Terry. In Pursuit of Excellence.
Oswald, Yvonne. Every Word has Power.
Robbins, Anthony., Awaken The Giant Within.
Robbins Blair, Forbes., Instant self-Hypnosis.
Royle, Dr Jonathan., Confessions of a Hypnotist.
Waterfield, Robin., Hidden Depths.

Notes

SELF-HYPNOSIS FOR SOCCER

DISCLAIMER

Neither PAUL M MAHER nor MIND TRAINING ARENA will be held responsible for any accident or misadventure arising from the improper use of information laid out in this manual. This manual is written specifically for someone to learn self-hypnosis, not as tuition to hypnotise others.

Introduction

Sport hypnosis can be a vital psychological tool to assist soccer players to get the best of themselves in training and competition and will improve their abilities, so they can achieve the wishes they long for to the exclusion of all other critical, negative or distracting influences which may otherwise create doubt in their ability.

When the player is in the relaxed, receptive state hypnosis brings, the critical faculties of the conscious mind are suspended, enabling the player to become receptive to positive suggestions. They can see themselves successfully executing skills, moves, or the other experiences they train for. Even if the player is limited in physical activity because of injury, they can remain positive and overcome any negative mindset, maintain their sense of purpose, keep passion for soccer alive and overcome any distress.

Lets take it one easy step at a time. To begin, there are many myths about hypnosis, often undeserved, which I should clear up. Its not magical, nor does it give someone magic powers. Nor can it turn you into Superman otherwise we would all be flying around. You cannot get 'stuck' in hypnosis, you do not put yourself under someone's 'power' who will then take control of you. You cannot become possessed. You cannot be made to do something which is against your moral code. You do not leave your body, you do not lose your mind.

Hollywood and the media thrives on drama and many stories in books and on film are the child of fertile imaginations as people lose control at the hands of the evil hypnotist to heighten tension in the story line. Those writers themselves have probably been influenced by a previous writers mistaken idea of what hypnosis is about.

More of the misunderstandings come from stage hypnosis shows. Here the participants are in full agreement to the suggestions they have been given. Those people on stage are volunteers who are fully prepared to go along with the entertainment. And that's all it is, entertainment.

Let me reassure you, hypnosis is a natural state of mind which can be used as an efficient psychological tool for a player to reach full potential. Self-hypnosis can be a great vehicle to get you into the performance zone.

Those easiest to hypnotise have the strongest, most creative minds with the greatest ability to use their concentration, imagination and intelligence. Very few people are not able to get into a hypnotic state and there is usually a reason. Epilepsy can create difficulty to focus, the really mentally subnormal, senility and those experiencing alcohol or drug abuse.

With clinical hypnosis, I am not going to get you barking like a dog, that's not going to cure your first touch, or help you maintain your goal scoring record. Hypnosis is a reliable, therapeutic method recognised by orthodox medicine.

Here you will discover how to help yourself achieve success in soccer. Surprisingly you have been in hypnosis many, many times before, although you may not realise it. A regular journey to work for example, when you realise you do not remember getting there. Don't worry about anything like that though, your subconscious is on constant duty 24 hours a day making sure you are safe. As soon as conscious attention is needed, your subconscious gets you there instantly.

How about reading when you realise you have not noticed a single word because your mind has been someplace else, so you have to re-read the whole thing again. Or you're watching a film and you don't realise someone is talking to you until they start shouting to get your attention – because you have been absorbed with the story on the screen.

These are all forms of hypnosis which happen to you everyday. The examples show you were focused, however on something else.

Some clients think they failed to 'go under' as nothing more than extreme relaxation took place. They knew they could move or open their eyes if they wanted to, they were just too comfortable to be bothered. That is what hypnosis can be for some people. The best way to describe what you may experience, is remember how you feel just moments before actual sleep occurs, or moments before you wake up. At that moment you pass through a state very similar to hypnosis.

Here are some of the sensations you may experience, its different for everybody:

Extremely relaxed
Floaty
Tingling in the hands or features
Feeling either light or heavy
More awareness, senses heightened
Warmth or cold
Stress free

Preparation

I'm going to teach you a preparation routine which I would like you to practice. This has been adapted from the self-hypnosis script by Terrence Watts of Hypnosense who has many more scripts. Do it with your eyes open a few times so you can read yourself through it, it's easy to remember.

Make sure you won't be disturbed for about ten minutes and visit the toilet before you begin. Sit comfortably. Some people prefer a straight-backed chair to an armchair. Have both your feet flat on the floor so there is good circulation down to your toes and place your hands relaxed in your lap. There is a position where your head feels as if it has no weight. Find that position where your head is weightless and so exactly aligned over your body so that your breathing is at its best.

Exercise

Close your eyes and remember a feeling of ease and peace drifting down through your body, relaxing every muscle. If you find that difficult, imagine how it would feel if your muscles were relaxed. Slow your breathing right down so that your breathing so gently, you wouldn't disturb a feather placed near your nose.

Don't rush it. Relaxation comes in its own time. After a while, you will feel yourself becoming calmer, quieter, your mind as still as your body. Its even fine if you notice your more aware than ever before. Stay with it.

And open your eyes when your ready.

How was that? You can actually go into hypnosis with that simple routine. You may have been surprised at just how easy images can form.

Visualisation

You should practice and become good at visualisation as it will lead you to success in your aims and goals. Some people think they cannot visualise anything as they cannot 'see' pictures in their minds eye. You don't have to see something exactly as if you were looking at a photograph. Try this. Remember a very short journey you did today. Something as simple as going from your front door to your living room. Imagine in your mind starting out and finishing it. Whatever it was, that's a visualisation for you.

Effective visualisation practice should use more of your senses than visual imagery. This way your other senses can be strengthened. Imagine what coffee smells like? How about freshly cut grass? Can you hear a whistle or crowd applause? What does your hair feel like? Don't touch it, imagine it.

Once you get used to it, you will soon be able to imagine every smell you can think of, any sound you have ever heard, any texture you have felt. Practice, smell things, feel things, listen to sounds.

Exercise

This time, find somewhere comfortable to sit where you won't be disturbed for twenty minutes or so. Put to one side any problems you are having to deal with, they'll still be there when you come back.

In fact, after some mental work, you may be able to deal with them more efficiently. One easy trick is to visualise a box or even a kit bag where you can place all your mental and emotional difficulties until you have time to sort them out.

Go through the preparation routine as before and when you are ready, recall some ordinary event that's happened in the last day or so. Remember your senses. How did it look? How did it sound? How did it feel? How did it smell or taste?

With practice, your memories will become more detailed. These images, when used in hypnosis, provide an edge to creating maximum success as you shall see.

Lets get into self hypnosis.

Self-Hypnosis

You should now be comfortable with the preparation and visualisation routines as I'm going to explain to you a three-part routine for getting into the hypnotic state.

But first, how do you come out of self-hypnosis? Simply finish the session by telling yourself to do so. Tell yourself you will be wide awake and alert, feeling fine on the count of five, then count yourself up from one to five and open your eyes. Practice that a few times.

Part 1

Close your eyes. Bring to mind a special day that you have had, even a great day out. Fun with friends, a walk in nature, relaxing on the beach. Notice how the memory starts, remember it and store it in your mind, you will use it later. Bring all your senses in now, remembering what you saw, what you heard, what you felt, even what you smelt and tasted if they are relevant.

Make everything real in your mind and keep focused until you can almost re-live one or more of those senses. It will often be the visual one, but don't let it concern you if you don't get it exact, it takes practice. As long as you have an awareness something is there is fine enough. Allow it to happen rather than force it to happen.

Part 2

With your eyes closed, imagine you are breathing peace into every cell of your body, each and every fibre of your being. And with every exhalation, you are letting go of any tension. Let each and every muscle from your head to your toes go limp as you exhale and repeat the word 'relax.' After half a dozen or so breaths, let yourself imagine you are drifting further down and you are becoming more relaxed, more than you have ever been. If you feel yourself floating up, just go with that.

Part 3

Remember in Part 1 storing the memory of a perfect day? You can use that now as a trigger for getting into self-hypnosis. This is best achieved after getting some practice with the first two parts. To use this trigger is very simple. After doing the preparation routine (it gets easier and faster the more you practice) and once your settled using Part 2, bring your happy memory to mind and let it help you drift down into trance – its that easy.

When you're ready, count yourself out.

I or You

There are countless ways to achieve self-hypnosis, the method I have shown you is just one. When you're in, read a prepared script or use a tape recorder to give yourself your desires. Its best to work on one thing at a time.

Its usual for people to say "I will," "I can," "I'm going to." This may be fine for you, but some people respond better by being told what to do, such as "you will," "you can," "your going to." It doesn't matter what you use, "I" or "you," as long as you use the form that feels right for you. If your unsure, make a script or recording using both versions to see which one you better respond to, just don't mix the two up together.

Reading a script is as good as making a recording once you get yourself into hypnosis. Have you ever been so absorbed in a book you lost all sense of time? Someone spoke to you and you didn't notice? That's hypnosis. Once your in hypnosis just tell yourself you will open your eyes and start reading following Part 3, read, then at the end of the script, close your eyes ready to count yourself up. For either script or recording, you may enjoy some quiet relaxation music playing in the background.

Now I'll show you how to use the state of hypnosis to achieve mastery.

Uses

Lets look how to actually use self-hypnosis to achieve your goals and desires.

Be sure you are now used to getting into and out of hypnosis. If not, your efforts will be wasted. I cannot repeat this enough, you must have a full grasp how to do it. The direct suggestions you will give yourself have to be compounded, so practice until its so ingrained, it will be an automatic response.

You will always be aware of sounds as you are not asleep, so simply relax. So if anything noisy happens outside, you're covered. Any sound you hear will not affect or disturb you, in fact, you can actually use any sound to deepen the trance. If there is heavy traffic outside, just tell yourself that all the traffic noise will help you to be more comfortable, deeper relaxed.

Caution

At the start of the session always tell yourself you will awake immediately if your full attention is needed for any emergency as a safety device. A further caution is not to drive or operate any machinery during your self-hypnosis session as it can slow down reflexes.

You can feel better, change habits, learn, block pain and so much more. Just decide what goal you need. For setting your goals, there are four 'must' rules which apply to every goal:

Plausible & Realistic

You nor I are magicians. If you are seventy years old you will not play in a Cup Final. If its not possible without hypnosis, its not possible with. If you cannot control the pace of your passes, then hypnosis will not create instant mastery for you. However, hypnosis can get you to the highest standard possible for you to produce those passes.

Suitable for Personality

For your goal to succeed, it should reflect your personality. Although hypnosis allows people to behave in a way which is different from their 'norm,' that's only temporary, so is no good for long-term goals. Select a goal which would not surprise a family member that you were doing it, then use hypnosis to speed up the process and become proficient at it.

Make it Clear

You need to know what it is that you want. Many people say "I want to be a winner." Ok, a winner at what? Your subconscious has the mind of a seven year old, it only works with uncomplicated, simple statements, not ambiguous ones. "I want to score at least five hat-tricks every season" is a clear goal. That is achievable.

Make it Positive

Think of what you want, not what you don't want. What you can do, not what you can't. What you like, not what you don't like. "I don't overlap enough" is not a positive statement. "I wish to overlap more and competently" is. By implication, consciously they mean the same to you, but the literal understanding subconscious does not understand implications. "I am determined not to miss an open goal" is a negative statement. "I am determined to score into an open goal if the opportunity arrives," carries a different message to your subconscious, which can only function on **what IS**, not understanding **what IS NOT**.

THE FOUR SENSES TEST

You should apply at least four of your senses to your visualisation of any goal. You should SEE yourself doing it successfully, receiving a reward perhaps; HEAR something associated with it, applause maybe; FEEL something associated, how about the cool metal of that trophy in your hands and then SMELL or TASTE something there, celebratory Champagne for example.

Now turn all of that into a living video, make it a rich, sense filled experience you can go over and over in your mind. As you practice using your senses, you will expand your conscious awareness.

Its best to work on one goal at a time, each goal can run into the next as you progress. Working on one goal at a time makes it more likely for you to achieve it and is a lot easier than trying to remember a jumble of scenarios.

Get yourself into hypnosis and be patient, you cannot hurry it. Once there, play your video in your mind three, four, five times and let yourself feel the excitement of this adventure each time. That's an emotional reward for yourself and is an important part of the success plan, so make it your reality.

Each time you do self-hypnosis, you will do it better than the time before. Want it to happen, let it happen.

You now have skill to improve your soccer.

Did you enjoy that? Visit www.mindtrainingarena.com

Enjoy your soccer.

Published in 2011 by Antony Rowe Publishing
48-50 Birch Close
Eastbourne
East Sussex
BN23 6PE
arp@cpi-group.co.uk

© PAUL M MAHER 2011

The Right of Paul M Maher to be identified as the Author of this work has been asserted by him in accordance with the Copyright, Designs and Patents Act 1988.

All Rights Reserved. No part of this book may be printed, reproduced or utilized in any form or by any electronic, mechanical or other means, now known or hereafter invented, including photocopying and recording, or in any information storage retrieval system, without permission in writing from the publishers.

A catalogue record for this book is available from the British Library

ISBN 978-1-907571-09-1

Printed and Bound in Great Britain by
CPI Antony Rowe, Chippenham and Eastbourne